Why We're Not Benefit Scroungers

Life with chronic illness or disability in modern Britain

Stef Benstead writing as

Aida Aleksia

Why We're Not Benefit Scroungers

Life with chronic illness or disability in modern Britain

ISBN: 978-0-9574597-0-0

This book is published by Aleksia Publishing in conjunction with **WRITERSWORLD**, and is produced entirely in the UK. It is available to order from most bookshops in the United Kingdom, and is also globally available via UK based Internet book retailers.

Copy edited by Jeremy Renals
Cover design by Jag Lall

SignWriting® (front cover symbols) by Valerie Sutton. "SignWriting®", "SignWriter®", "SignBank®", "Sign-Symbol-Sequence®" and "DanceWriting®" are trademarks belonging to the Center For Sutton Movement Writing, Inc.

WRITERSWORLD
2 Bear Close Flats, Bear Close, Woodstock
Oxfordshire, OX20 1JX, England
☎ 01993 812500
☎ +44 1993 812500

www.writersworld.co.uk

The text pages of this book are produced via an independent certification process that ensures the trees from which the paper is produced come from well managed sources that exclude the risk of using illegally logged timber while leaving options to use post-consumer recycled paper as well.

Dedicated to

Dr John Patterson

with thanks.

Acknowledgements

Thank you to everyone who so kindly let me use your stories as memoirs in this book.

Thank you to my family and friends who read the early manuscripts.

A huge thank you to the team at Writersworld: Graham Cook, Jeremy Renals and Jag Lall.

To all of you, thank you for the help, advice and work that you put in to making this book real.

Contents

Part 1: Benefit Britain?

Part 2: Life in the Slow Lane

Part 1

Benefit Britain?

Glossary of Acronyms and Initialisms

AA	Attendance Allowance
DLA	Disability Living Allowance
DWP	Department for Work and Pensions
ESA	Employment and Support Allowance
HCP	Health care professional
IB	Incapacity Benefit
PCA	Personal Capability Assessment
PIP	Personal Independence Payment
WCA	Work Capability Assessment

Summary of Part One

Introduction: The Beveridge Principle

The benefits system, as designed by Beveridge, should provide subsistence income for all who need it (due to job loss, ill health or other reasons).

It should itself generate the finances necessary for everyone to be insured against interruption of earnings.

The government should see rising welfare bills as an indication of the need to invest in other policies e.g. improved health care and job creation.

Chapter 1 The Cost of Disability

Disability brings numerous costs, e.g. difficulty with access to public transport, buildings and spaces, costs of housing, heating and maintenance, aids and adaptations, impact on education and ability to work, medication, treatment and support.

Private insurance cannot efficiently or effectively cover medical risks. This is why we need a social scheme to protect against loss of income and/or increases in expenditure due to ill health or disability.

Chapter 2 Government Misinformation

Escalating Costs

67% of benefits expenditure goes to pensioners.

More money is spent on health and on education than on benefits for people of working-age.

Working-age benefits fell from 1995/96 to 2000/01. It then rose a small amount to 2008/09, and his risen more since then due at least in part to the recession.

Increases in DLA (Disability Living Allowance) are explained by an ageing population and increases in numbers of claimants with mental health or learning difficulties. This is in line with the increase in prevalence of these conditions across developed countries.

Festering on Benefits?

Disabled and chronically ill people experience difficulty with access to education, public buildings and transport, and jobs.

Only 28% of people found 'fit for work' are in work 12-18 months later.

Work is Good for You?

ESA (Employment and Support Allowance) has one of the toughest assessment processes in the world.

Work brings health benefits only if it is well paid, stimulating, encourages personal development and has autonomy.

There is a significant minority for whom work makes their health worse.

Fraud?

Any assessment process has false positive and false negative decisions.

Fraud in health-related benefits is small, at 1 in every 2-300 claims.

Public perception of fraud is that it is very high; this is not an accurate perception.

Chapter 3 ESA and the WCA

ESA is the successor to Incapacity Benefit, Severe Disability Allowance and Income Support on grounds of health.

It is assessed through a questionnaire, medical assessment (WCA or Work Capability Assessment) and supporting information.

Claimants may be found fit for work, unfit for work but fit for work-related activity, or unfit for work and work-related activity.

Those found capable of work-related activity go in the Work Related Activity Group, and are expected to undertake work-related activity in return for their benefit. This includes things like attending work-focussed interviews, going on work placements and experience and attending courses at the Jobcentre.

Those found incapable of work-related activity go in the Support Group and do not have to carry out any actions in order to receive benefit.

DWP (the Department for Work and Pensions) have contracted out the WCA to Atos. Details of this contract are not available due to confidentiality.

Atos is a multi-national IT company. Atos healthcare employs doctors, nurses and physiotherapists to assess ESA claimants' ability to work.

Nurses and physiotherapists make up over 70% of these health care professionals (as full-time equivalents).

Only doctors can assess neurological conditions.

There has been a suggestion that the knowledge base of these health care professionals (HCPs) is not adequate.

Medical notes are not used in the assessment process.

Evidence submitted by the claimant's medical professionals may be used, but it is not compulsory for such evidence to be submitted.

LiMA, the computer programme used in the WCA, is based around a series of drop-down boxes and automated suggestions.

Incorrect selections made early in the assessment are propagated through the rest of the assessment report.

More recently, HCPs have been encouraged to use the free text boxes to create more individualised reports.

Lateral questions make it difficult to obtain accurate or reliable information on a claimant's state of health and ability to work. Answers to one question are used as answers to more demanding questions that were not asked.

There seems to be a mismatch between the language used by the DWP, Atos staff and decision makers compared to language used by the claimants.

The descriptors used to assess ability to work seem to be too narrow.

Atos centres are frequently inaccessible in a variety of ways to disabled and chronically ill people.

Decisions on ESA claims are made by non-medical staff at the DWP. Quality of decision-making by these people is highly variable, as identified by Professor Harrington.

The assessment process is too close to being a medical model. It does not take into account many of the barriers presented by society.

The process is frequently inaccurate:

- Of 37 reports, 16 were substantially incorrect and only 10 had no or low inaccuracy.
- 41% of people found fit for work go on to appeal. Of these, 34% win; the figure is higher at 70-100% if the claimant has a representative.
- 60% of appeals won by claimants were for cases where the claimant was initially awarded zero points. 23% has 3-6 points, and 17% had 7-14 points (15 is the cut-off for ESA).

There is concern that the ESA assessment process does not adequately take into account mental health or fluctuating illnesses.

Chapter 4: DLA and PIP

Disability Living Allowance is not an out-of-work benefit. It is a benefit paid to disabled people to help them with the cost of living with a disability.

It is not means-tested and does not have any restrictions on how it can be used.

The current assessment process is carried out by means of a detailed questionnaire and evidence from the claimant's medical professionals.

Claimants may get higher or lower rate mobility, and/or higher, middle or lower rate care.

Higher rate mobility is for people who are unable or virtually unable to walk. Usually a person must be in receipt of this benefit to get a Blue Badge.

Lower rate mobility is for people who need guidance or supervision when in unfamiliar outdoor places.

Lower rate care is for people who need attention for bodily functions for a significant proportion of the day or (if over 16) cannot prepare a cooked meal from fresh ingredients.

Middle rate care is for those who need frequent attention or constant supervision during either the day or the night.

Higher rate care is for those who need frequent attention or constant supervision during both the day and the night.

DLA replaced Attendance Allowance, because it was recognised that the face-to-face interview was a large source of errors in decision making.

60% of DLA claims are turned down initially. Appeal success runs at 45%, rising to 67% when there is a representative present.

DLA fraud results in overpayments of 0.5% of the total expenditure. Customer error is 0.6% and official error is 0.8%.

A rise in DLA claims recently is in part due to pensioners claiming DLA and partly due to increased prevalence of mental health and learning difficulties.

DLA is not a disincentive to work and in many cases is the means by which a person can work, e.g. by paying for taxis to work.

The government is removing automatic entitlement for many groups. Currently automatic entitlement goes to the following groups: severe visual impairment; 80% deaf and 100% blind; severe mental impairment; double amputees; renal dialysis carried out at home; and less than 6 months to live.

Aids to disability living can be expensive and need maintenance. This should be factored in to plans for reform to DLA.

The government's plan to cut 20% from DLA expenditure suggests an *a priori* decision, not one based on the needs of the people concerned.

The new PIPs (Personal Independence Payments), the replacement for DLA, should be based on a social model of disability and not a medical model.

Need is not an accurate measure of cost, and so to focus on the 'most needy' may not result in an appropriate or well-designed replacement for DLA.

The government may face human rights issues over its changes to DLA, in part because "The duty of progressive realisation in UN human rights treaties entails a strong presumption against retrogressive measures affecting the right to social security and to an adequate standard of living." The changes to DLA may bring negative impacts on the right of disabled people to independent living.

Introduction: The Beveridge Principle

During the Second World War, the then Labour-Conservative coalition government asked William Beveridge to carry out a survey on social insurance in Britain. An inter-departmental committee was formed, with the mandate to "undertake, with special reference to the inter-relation of the schemes, a survey of the existing national schemes of social insurance and allied services, including workmen's compensation, and to make recommendations." That is, Beveridge and his committee were asked to look at what measures were in place to provide for people in poverty, to help them to move out of poverty, and to see what practices were in place to protect against loss of earnings during job-loss or ill-health. Beveridge also recognised that some people would never be able to earn because of the state of their health, and it was plain that these people would also be provided for.

In November 1942, Beveridge presented the *Report of the Inter-Departmental Committee on Social Insurance and Allied Services*, commonly known as the Beveridge report, to the government. Beveridge's first principle was that, "Now, when the war is abolishing landmarks of every kind, is the opportunity for using experience in a clear field. A revolutionary moment in the world's history is a time for revolutions, not for patching." He was also clear that income security was not the only provision the government should make; the government also had to act against Disease, Ignorance, Squalor and Idleness.

In abolishing Want, Beveridge insisted that current social insurance schemes needed to improve. "To prevent interruption or destruction of earning power from leading to Want, it is necessary to improve the present schemes of social insurance in three directions: by extension of scope to cover persons now excluded, by extension of purposes to cover risks now excluded, and by raising the rates of benefit."

Throughout the report, Beveridge insisted that benefit rates should be sufficient to cover subsistence. He was committed to the idea that "Social Insurance should aim at guaranteeing the minimum income needed for subsistence," such that, "The scheme of Social Insurance is designed of itself when in full operation to guarantee the income needed for subsistence in all normal cases."[1] Beveridge considers that a minimum income for everyone is a necessity. Whilst he agrees that state aid "should not stifle incentive, opportunity, responsibility," he clearly considers that provision of a minimum income does not lead to such stifling. He also considers that, rather than penalise the long-term disabled and jobless in order to cut costs, the government should view rising welfare costs as an indicator of its need to invest in job creation and improved medical aid. Such a view would ensure that there is access to support for all who need it, whilst not trapping people on benefits because of an overarching economical principle that has not ensured sufficient jobs for the general working-age population, and sufficient accessible jobs for the disabled.

Squalor and Disease were linked. Squalor referred to the inability of the poor to pay for medical care, resulting in their being unable to recover and return to work. This also led to a reduction in the labour force. Disease similarly causes financial trouble, as sickness forces a cessation in work. With the recent germ theory of Disease and the Public Health Act of 1875, Beveridge was able to recommend the creation of the National Health Service, which provided free medical aid to everyone in Britain.

Interestingly, the biggest issue with Ignorance was not lack of general education. In a cartoon from the time entitled 'Tackling the First Giant,' "the worst manifestation of Ignorance is depicted as bigoted small mindedness"[2] on the part of the wealthy. The implication was clear, and

---

[1] Sir William Beveridge, Report of the Inter-Departmental Committee on Social Insurance and Allied Services, November 1942 [Beveridge Report]

[2] Danny Dorling, 2010, Social Evils – From Unemployment to Idleness to Prejudice. Review of Economics 2

similar to French President Hollande's statement that the 75% tax on income above €1 million should be seen as 'patriotic.' "It is patriotic to agree to pay a supplementary tax to get the country back on its feet."[3]

With the end of the war and election of a new Labour government under Clement Attlee, new social policies were brought in that became the Welfare State. They included child benefit, unemployment and sickness benefits, widow benefit and a retirement pension. The aim was to have a comprehensive social insurance system "from cradle to grave." The National Health Service began in 1948, under a Conservative government led by Churchill. This gave free diagnosis and treatment, including dental and ophthalmic care, which are now only partially subsidised by the state. "It shall be the duty of the Minister of Health ... to promote the establishment ... of a comprehensive health service designed to secure improvement in the physical and mental health of the people of England and Wales and the prevention, diagnosis and treatment of illness, and for that purpose to provide or secure the effective provision of services."

For many, this is still the welfare state that we expect. We expect that when we are ill, we will get treatment (although we may have to wait for it!). We expect that if we are made redundant, the state will help us, through Jobseeker's Allowance, until we are able to find another position. We expect that if we become ill, and remain so for more than 28 weeks when Statutory Sick Pay ends, we again will be helped financially until we are back in paid work. We know that when we have children we get money towards their upkeep, and that when we retire we get a state pension.

The idea is that those who are 'deserving' get the support they need. Most people currently in employment consider themselves 'deserving.' Along the lines of, I've paid my National Insurance, so I should get all the help I need. Mental distinctions are made between the 'deserving' and 'undeserving' poor and sick, which allows

[3] as cited in BBC News, 28th February 2012, French election: Hollande wants 75% tax on top earners.

for the labelling of others as cheats, scroungers and fakers. This is often done without knowing the details of any individual case, and so allows us to have an 'Oh, I don't mean people like you' attitude on the rare occasions when we do know the circumstances behind a person's current jobless state.

Fundamentally, we expect that those who are deserving do get the support that they need, and that we in turn will get support if life circumstances render it necessary. We expect that those who are feckless and lazy will not be supported. It is on the basis that a large proportion of people on benefits are feckless and lazy that the government proposes and the public supports a cut in the welfare bill and a reform in the methodology underpinning the benefits system. Whilst the Guardian largely writes pieces that are supportive of those on benefits, most other media providers are more in line with the government's rhetoric of the culture of worklessness and money wasted on cheats.

Rhetoric, whether kind or condemning to those on benefits, is not helpful. What is helpful is to know the facts, reach conclusions based on them and develop policy based on them. With that in mind, this book aims to present the facts with minimal rhetoric. The facts can speak well enough for themselves.

This book contains some of the facts about the welfare system as it relates to the disabled and unwell. It also reports stories from some of those whose health is not all that might be desired, and how this impacts their lives. There are costs to ill health, which those who have no experience of such things would not know about. There are difficulties with life, education and work which go beyond the symptoms. These stories are shared with you in the hope that, through reading them, you will come to understand more about what it means to be disabled or sick in this country.

The government and media often conflate Disability Living Allowance (DLA) and Employment and Support Allowance (ESA):

- DLA is not an out-of-work benefit. Rather, it is a payment made to those whose health condition means they have expensive medical needs. The payment of DLA is often the means that allows disabled and unwell people to work. Currently it is not means-tested.
- ESA is an out-of-work benefit. It is paid to those people whose health is too poor for them to work or look for work. People who have paid sufficient National Insurance can claim ESA for a year; after this, ESA is only paid if the person is sufficiently poor. Anyone with a partner who earns more than £7500 a year will not receive ESA.

As the government seeks to save money, it is important that the public is fully informed about the nature and impacts of the cuts being made. Often, the unwell are described as scroungers and fraud is estimated as a huge problem. However, the reality is very different. I hope that by reading this, you will be able to make an informed decision on whether or not the government is correct to cut support for chronically ill or disabled people.

1

The Cost of Disability

"General saving is really important to us," he says. *"We are a nation that doesn't save ... We drifted into a culture where consumption was all, and you borrowed to spend ... So we change the culture so that you save, you invest and you prepare for the worst. Like we insure our cars, this is basically insuring our lives."*[4] - Iain Duncan Smith, MP for Chingford and Wooding Green, and Secretary of State for Work and Pensions.

Which sounds great. Insure your life, then if (when) bad times come, the insurance will pay out to keep you safe. This is what National Insurance was introduced for. It is what private health or life insurance contributes towards. But life, unlike owning and insuring a vehicle, is not a luxury. If you are poor, you can choose not to own a car (although this reduces job access, further contributing to your poverty). But few people consider that the alternative to insurance for the poor should be for them to choose not to live.

Most people don't spend time reflecting on how they will manage if they fall ill. Is the mortgage on the house affordable if you develop lupus and can no longer work? Can you raise two children if you lose your sight? Will you be able to care for your ageing parents if you have a stroke and become hemiplegic? Should you avoid all holidays abroad, in order to save up money to ensure you can tide yourself and your family over when the tide goes out on your health? Do you live in the smallest house you can fit your family into, live in the cheapest area you can, own the most economical car, deny yourself all luxuries – so that on

---

[4] Iain Duncan Smith, MP for Chingford and Wooding Green, and Secretary of State for Work and Pensions. In The Telegraph, Iain Duncan Smith: I'm not afraid to light the fuse on disability reform, 13th May 2012, Robert Winnett

the day when the stroke strikes, the heart attack attacks or your memory walks out and forgets to return, you have enough savings that you do not ever need to ask for support from a charity, friend or government?

Private insurers operate by pooling risk for a group of similar people. If there is a 1 in 100 risk of having goods stolen from your house in a given year, insurance means each of the 100 homeowners pays an insurance company to remunerate them if they are the one that is burgled. The alternative would be for each homeowner to have enough money invested that, in the event of being burgled, all stolen goods can be replaced. This is highly inefficient, because in reality there only needs to be one set of money to replace stolen goods, not 100.

People at high risk of a particular costly event are charged more, because it is more likely that they will need to make a claim. If you lived in an area where 1 in 20 houses had goods stolen each year, your insurance would be a lot higher; for every 100 houses there would then need to be 5 sets of remuneration money. At the far end, people become uninsurable and it is unreasonable to expect private insurers, who need to make money and ensure they can pay out on small or infrequent claims, to pay out for the expenses of this group.

The same principles hold for all insured items, whether personal goods, health, or anything else. In particular, some groups of people are more susceptible to certain (potentially costly) illnesses than others. Private insurers won't, and can't be expected to, insure these people. This is where National Insurance comes in. National Insurance (technically not insurance in the way that private insurance works) is a way of ensuring that everyone is protected against loss of income through ill-health (or redundancy, or any other interruption to earning). National Insurance is necessary if a country wishes to ensure that people suffering misfortune are not also condemned to suffering penury. Only the state can provide this sort of protection. Neither individuals nor private companies can afford to do this, and it would be highly inefficient for them to do so.

Living with disability or chronic illness is costly. That is why support is needed. Whether in work or not, disability brings additional costs to life that the disabled person may not be able to meet. Disability and chronic illness can hinder education, employment and access, as well as bringing medical costs.

In a 2009 study, it was found that more than a quarter of disabled people had had problems accessing public transport in the previous twelve months; of these, 58% had found stations or terminals inaccessible, and 64% found the mode of transport inaccessible.[5] This study concluded that "inaccessible transport continues to be one of the biggest barriers to social inclusion experienced by disabled people, restricting employment options, limiting access to healthcare and obstructing participation in social networks and communities." This means that despite the requirement for transport service providers to make reasonable adjustments, public transport remains largely inaccessible. For example, only 66 of London tube stations are accessible (in terms of completely step free access between the street, platform and carriage),[6] and Transport for London is not putting any money towards improving accessibility in the next few years.

Housing is another large cost for disabled people. This includes finding suitable accommodation (e.g. bungalows, for the same floor space, are more expensive) and adapting accommodation to needs. If overnight carers are needed then an extra bedroom will have to be paid for. Heating is often a larger cost for disabled people who may struggle to keep warm. Electricity bills may also be higher, especially if frequent washing of laundry and/or tumble dryers are required.

Other costs come from household maintenance. With social care funding being cut there are ever fewer services provided by social care workers. This can leave disabled people having to pay privately for help with shopping,

---

[5] Greenhalgh and Gore, 2009, Disability Review, Leonard Cheshire Disability.

[6] http://www.tfl.gov.uk/gettingaround/transportaccessibility/1169.aspx

tidying, cleaning, laundry and other such household chores.

Costs continue when a person is in employment. This is often through the high cost of private transport. Other costs are incurred when working leaves a disabled person unable to carry out household tasks, and therefore paying for these to be done.

The educational levels of disabled people are significantly lower than non-disabled people. At the ages of 18-19, 28% of non-disabled people lack NVQ Level 1 (GCSE grades D-G), but for disabled people it is almost 50%. At 16-17, disabled people are less likely to be in full-time education. Post-16, disabled people are less likely to get the education, training or job they want.[7] A study from Ireland found that as the severity and duration of disability increased, the likelihood of having any given qualification was reduced.[8] In London, disabled young people are twice as likely as non-disabled to not be in education, employment or training (NEET).[9]

This is not due to lack of aspiration.[10] At 16, disabled and non-disabled young people had similar aspirations. The difference was that by 26, disabled people were much less likely to have achieved theirs.

Even having reached the same education levels, disabled people are at a disadvantage. A disabled person with a degree is less likely to be in employment than a non-disabled person who has 5 GCSEs (A* - C).[11] Whilst some disabled people are unable to work because of the nature of their condition, disabled people still form a large proportion - almost half - of unemployed people who want

---

[7] Burchadt, 2005, The Education and Employment of Disabled Young People, Joseph Rowntree Foundation

[8] ibid., Chapter 3 Disability and Education

[9] Baker, Findlay, Murage, Pettitt, Leeser, Goldblatt, Fitzpatrick, and Jacobson, 2011, Fair London, Healthy Londoners? London Health Commission, Greater London Authority

[10] Burchadt, 2005, The Education and Employment of Disabled Young People, JRF.

[11] Aldridge, Parekh, MacInnes and Kenway, 2011, Monitoring Poverty and Social Exclusion,. JRF

to work.[12] They also earn 11% less than a non-disabled person with the same level of qualification.[13] Lack of promotion and training opportunities for disabled people create more indirect costs.[14] The Joseph Rowntree report concludes, "A reasonable inference from these figures is that the collective action of employers means that once allowance is made for level of qualifications, the opportunities for disabled workers are different from those for non-disabled ones. Irrespective of employer intentions, this has the effect of being discriminatory."

Disabled people often want to work and aspire to work as much as any non-disabled person. But their health, combined with lack of accessibility in society, effectively discriminates against them.

Poverty amongst disabled people is common. Almost half of households with a disabled member are in the bottom 40% of the income distribution (after housing costs). For non-disabled households this is less than a third. Moreover, 29% of disabled households are in poverty, compared to 17% for non-disabled households. In London, 73% of households with one disabled adult do not reach the minimum income standard, and this rises to 80% if there are two disabled adults; for non-disabled households it is just 43%.[15]

We must remember that income measures alone do not cover the true extent of poverty for disabled households, because they do not acknowledge the additional costs incurred by disabled people because of their disabilities.

---

[12] Disability Rights Commission, 2004 http://www.official-documents.gov.uk/document/hc0506/hc02/0253/0253.asp

[13] Burchadt, 2005, The Education and Employment of Disabled Young People, JRF

[14] Berthoud, Lakey and McKay, 1993, The Economic Problems of Disabled People, London: Policy Studies Institute; Yelin, 1998, The economics of osteoarthritis, in Brandt, Doherty and Lohmander (Eds) *Osteoarthritis* Oxford University Press; both as quoted in JRF 2004 Disabled People's Costs of Living

[15] Fair London, Healthy Londoners?, Baker, Findlay, Murage, Pettitt, Leeser, Goldblatt, Fitzpatrick, and Jacobson, 2011, London Health Commission, Greater London Authority

Up to 60% of disabled people may be in poverty once these costs have been taken into account.[16] JRF (the Joseph Rowntree Foundation) conclude that, "if up to 60 per cent of disabled people experience income poverty, and if disabled people have additional costs that must be met from these incomes, questions must be raised about the adequacy of current state support."[17]

JRF made an assessment of the needs of disabled people. They estimated what these would cost, based on the average price of meeting these needs. Excluding personal assistance costs,[18] they found that the amount of benefit provided routinely falls £200 short of the amount needed each week. Whilst benefits meet 50% of the needs of those with high-medium needs, they fall short by £238; benefits meet 28% of low-medium needs, and fall £200 short. These are large shortfalls even when the maximum benefit is received, and without considerations of the cost of personal assistance. Even if a disabled person is employed,[19] and again without considering personal assistance costs, there are shortfalls of £118-£189 per week.

The Greater London Authority defines disabled people as "those who are prevented by barriers put up by society from taking part in aspects of everyday life on equal terms with not-disabled people." UK legislation confirms this definition of disability, as does the UN. UNESCO says that, "The greatest barriers to inclusion are caused by society,

---

[16] Zaidi and Burchadt, 2002, Comparing Incomes when Needs Differ: Equivalisation for the Extra Costs of Disability in the UK. Paper 64 London: Centre for Analysis of Social Exclusion

[17] Smith, Middleton, Ashton-Brooks, Cox, Dobson and Reith, 2004, Disabled People's Costs of Living, JRF

[18] Personal assistance costs include interpreters for deaf people, trainers for blind people, support for personal care and support with other domiciliary services.

[19] JRF assumes a 20 hr week on minimum wage, because of the strong links between qualifications and employment, qualifications and disability, and disability and employment; this is therefore a realistic example of possible wages.

not by particular impairments." These barriers include negative attitudes towards disabled people.[20]

The Greater London Authority recognises disablism, or disability discrimination, as a form of oppression. "Medical and associated interventions should in no way be seen as substituting for ongoing work to challenge and deal with barriers faced by disabled people in mainstream society... 'Equal opportunities' does not mean that all people are treated the same, but rather that their diversity is recognised and accommodated to enable them to access services and opportunities."[21] Beveridge, when he first reported on the need for the Welfare State, also agreed with this.

This disablism incurs multiple costs for disabled people, who may then have to pay for private rather than public transport; provide their own sign language interpreter; pay delivery charges for internet shopping; pay for what is most accessible rather than what is cheapest. The lack of accessibility of society adds to the costs that disabled people face.

Disabled people also face higher costs when their higher level of risk means they are charged more by private companies, such as higher premiums for insurance and mortgage facilities.

The Joseph Rowntree Foundation concluded: "Much could be achieved if society was properly attuned to the needs of disabled people and effectively enhanced services could do much to reduce the costs carried by individuals. At the same time, additional resources directly for individuals are also required in order to facilitate the 'level playing field' that disabled people seek.[22]"

---

[20] UNESCO, Barriers to Inclusive Education http://www.unescobkk.org/education/inclusive-education/what-is-inclusive-education/barriers-to-inclusive-education/

[21] Barer, Davies and Fitzpatrick. Review of the London Health Strategy high-level indicators, Section 3, 2003, London Health Authority

[22] Smith, Middleton, Ashton-Brooks, Cox, Dobson and Reith, 2004, Disabled People's Costs of Living, JRF

Unless the government recognises this, people with impairments or chronic illnesses will continue to face discrimination from, and be disabled by, society.

2

Government Misinformation

The rhetoric of a benefits system rife with cheats and scroungers is common in the British media and government. Pejorative language about the undeserving, feckless and lazy is used, and responded to, in a spiral of misinformation. It creates the idea that a large proportion of hard-working tax-payers' money goes to people who cannot be bothered to work themselves. The Prime Minister and Iain Duncan Smith talk about generations of workless families and cultures of worklessness. They talk about people receiving Incapacity Benefit or its successor, Employment and Support Allowance, as 'festering.' There is discussion of people 'abandoned' on benefits. And there is frequent reference to large numbers of people cheating the system.

Very little, if any, of this is true. As far as the disabled community is concerned, it is difficult to find any truth in what has been said about the community and the welfare bill.

Escalating costs

"As a result under the last Government, the amount spent on welfare was remarkable, increasing by 40% in real terms even in a decade of unprecedented growth and rising employment." [23]

The government, and much of the media, report the welfare bill as too high. They imply that people receiving benefit either do not need or do not deserve it. This belief – based on little, if any, evidence - is reflected amongst the public, three-quarters of whom agreed in a YouGov poll

[23] Iain Duncan Smith, 27th June 2012, Speech on welfare to the Ways and Means Committee, House of Congress.

that the government pays out too much in benefits.[24] Two-thirds think that a substantial minority or around a half of benefit recipients lie in order to get higher payments. In addition, 55% of the respondents thought they gave more to the government in tax than they receive back, whilst 37% either didn't know or thought it is roughly equal. Together these surveys show a mind-set of us against them: us, the tax-payers, not getting value for money; and them, the recipients of hard-working tax-payers money, who have no good claim to it.

These views are not based on or backed up by the facts. The majority of people in this country get more in return for their tax than they give to the government.[25] This means that most 'hard-working tax-payers' can be said to 'scrounge' off the government in the sense that they get more from the government than they pay in. The tax-payer/non-tax-payer dichotomy is also invalid; there are many taxes beyond Income Tax and Council Tax that will be paid by everyone. In consequence of all this, any us/them dichotomy should be between (as a rough guide) the top 25% and the bottom 75%, as this is where the cross-over from net recipient to net contributor occurs.

This us/them position also relies heavily on the assumption that a large proportion of those on benefits are 'undeserving,' often used to mean lazy; people choosing to live off benefits without seeking work. There is little data around this issue, and none for disabled or chronically ill people. What data there is suggests that benefits as a lifestyle choice is not common. Furthermore, with fraud in the health-related benefit system running at 1 in every 200-300,[26] it is unlikely that there are many 'undeserving' recipients of health-related benefits.

In the quote above, Iain Duncan Smith implies that money has been wasted on areas where it is not needed, or has been allowing people who could find work to instead

---

[24] Kellner, Monday 27th February, Charity ends at horme. YouGov, Prospect.

[25] See Appendix 1.

[26] Fraud and error in the benefit system, June 2012, DWP http://statistics.dwp.gov.uk/asd/asd2/index.php?page=fraud_error

choose a life on benefits. He implies that the welfare bill could be much smaller without making much negative impact on those who are 'deserving' or needy. But he fails to discuss where the welfare money was going. He therefore does not address the question of whether much of the welfare bill is money going to those not in need or deserving; he also does not address how many needy people will be driven further into need as a result of reductions in the welfare bill.

Most welfare payments do not go to those whom some people may class as 'undeserving.' In fact the majority go to pensioners; pensions made up 18% of the government spending bill in 2011 and are expected to increase to 20% in 2013.[27] The rest of welfare makes up 17% of the bill, although some of this also goes to pensioners. For comparison, health spending is 18% and education is 13%.

In terms of the increase in the welfare bill, over 50% of the increase under the last government went to pensioners – a group that is growing, and one for whom the argument about unprecedented growth and rising employment is irrelevant.[28] Tax credits form about one third of the increase. The other large component is Housing Benefit. Housing Benefit goes to a range of people, including pensioners (21%), those working less than 16 hours a week because of caring duties (23%), those in low-paid work (18%), and those who are too ill to work (at least 8%[29]).[30]

In 2010-11, working-age benefits costs 3.5% of GDP. This is similar to the level in the early 1980s and is smaller than the levels being paid through the 1990s, which peaked

[27] http://www.ukpublicspending.co.uk/total_spending_2011UKbn

[28] Gaffney, 5th July 2010, A ballooning welfare bill? It's not that simple, LabourList.

[29] This 8% refers to people on income-based Employment and Support Allowance; a further 17% receive either contribution based Jobseeker's Allowance or contribution based ESA, but the figures do not distinguish between the two.

[30] DWP data on HB recipients http://research.dwp.gov.uk/asd/asd1/hb_ctb/index.php?page=hbctb_arc

at 4.6%.[31] Spending on working-age benefits increased by less than £3 billion between 2000/01 and 2008/09, having first seen a fall from peak levels in 1995/96.[32] There has also been an increase between 2008/09 to 2010/11, from £46.6 billion to £53.4 billion; this increase is largely due to an increase in Jobseeker's Allowance and Housing Benefit as a consequence of the recession. Before the recession, benefits to working-age people contributed a mere 6% to the total increase since 2000/01. This "should dispose of any claims that structural problems in the social security system or the labour market are the major driver of the growth in welfare expenditure over the last ten years."[33]

The UK does compare well with other developed countries in terms of the amount spent on welfare, generally being average or slightly above average in terms of how much is spent as a percentage of GDP or per capita.[34] However, in terms of working-age benefits the UK has "low welfare reliance compared to other countries – lower than US apart from maternity benefits;" in particular its spending on incapacity is small compared to other developed countries.[35] Welfare reliance also decreased from the period around 1993/94 up to the recession, and the increase in the welfare bill between 2001/02 and the recession was the only time in which the increase was under control.

However if the government wishes to cut the welfare bill, it needs to focus on those benefits that form a large part of the bill and those that are not means-tested. It also needs to consider what alternative ways there are to

---

[31] Owen Spottiswoode, 'Inconvenient truth?' Has the UK's welfare bill grown sevenfold over the past half century? 27th September 2012 FullFact.

[32] Gaffney, 5th July 2010, A ballooning welfare bill? It's not that simple, LabourList.

[33] ibid.

[34] Social Protections and Expenditure, Data 1997-2005, European Social Statistics

[35] Gregg, 20th October 2012, Disability, Employment and Welfare Reform, Key Note Speech at 'The Hardest Hit': Disability research and welfare reform, Leeds. inequalitiesblog.files.wordpress.com/2012/09/gregg-leeds-disability.ppt

reduce the bill – for example, providing more state childcare, raising national minimum wage and ensuring that there is more affordable housing.

The government has pledged to not touch pensioners' benefits; a major flaw if the government wishes to cut benefits because this group takes up 67% of the welfare bill[36] and pensioners are the only group of people for whom means-tested benefits provide an adequate income.[37] Instead, the government has decided to cut 20% from the DLA bill; DLA comprises a mere 8% of the overall bill, and estimates by the Joseph Rowntree Foundation indicate that DLA payments are inadequate.[38]

In reference to rising costs in disability payments, David Turner says that, "The escalating cost of welfare is a real political challenge. However, this is the result of a rising population of disabled people due to higher survival rates rather than mounting fraud. It will remain difficult for the government to get its message across that reforms are intended to help the most vulnerable when media perceptions of the most vulnerable types reinforce negative stereotypes."[39]

The government has said that, "In just eight years the number claiming the benefit [DLA] has risen from around 2.5 million to nearly 3.2 million—an increase of nearly 30%.[40]" However 36% of this growth was from the

---

[36] April 2012, Social Security benefits and expenditure: social indicators, DWP

[37] Aldridge, Parekh, MacInnes and Kenway, 2011, Monitoring Poverty and Social Exclusion, Joseph Rowntree Foundation

[38] Smith, Middleton, Ashton-Brooks, Cox, Dobson and Reith, 2004, Disabled People's Costs of Living, JRF *See the chapter "The Cost of Disability."*

[39] David M Turner, February 2012, 'Fraudulent' disability in historical perspective, History and Policy

[40] DWP evidence submitted to Work and Pensions Committee http://www.publications.parliament.uk/pa/cm201012/cmselect/cmworpen/1493/1493we13.htm

increase in numbers of pensioners receiving DLA.[41] There has also been a large increase in children and young teenagers receiving DLA.[42] Neither pensioners nor children and young teenagers will be affected by the changes to DLA that the government is bringing in.

For DLA claims based on physical health, all of the increase since 2002 can be based on the increase in overall population size plus the demographic change, with increasing numbers of pensioners becoming eligible each year. The rest of the increase in claims since then is due to increased numbers of claimants with mental health issues or learning difficulties.[43] This matches the increasing prevalence of severe mental health issues and learning difficulties in all developed countries, and cannot therefore be attributed purely to any inappropriate loosening of criteria.

The government has ring-fenced money to the NHS and overseas-aid, although this may change. Helping people who are unwell or who are hugely disadvantaged by life is considered to be an important and morally right thing to do. So why, when it comes to helping our own sick and disadvantaged, is it satisfactory to cut 20% from the payments for DLA without any investigation into what impact this will have?

Whilst it is clear that the government needs to reduce the money it is spending, there are some expenditures that are basic necessities. No-one who lacks food, clean water, shelter from the elements or reasonable health can even begin to consider getting education or work. The government should not be cutting money to people in poverty, with disabilities or with poor health; this is a false economy that leads to more people needing more help from other services, such as the NHS.

---

[41] Pensioners only receive DLA if they were receiving DLA before retirement. If a person becomes chronically ill or disabled after retirement then that person claims Attendance Allowance, not DLA.

[42] http://touchstoneblog.org.uk/2011/08/why-are-there-more-dla-claimants/

[43] Campbell, Marsh, Franklin, Gaffney, Dixon, James, Barnett-Cormack, Fon-James, Willis, 2012, Responsible Reform

Festering on Benefits?

"What we will not do is put anyone on benefits and then forget about them, as was so frequently the case for those on sickness benefits in the UK."[44]

"For too long in this country we have left people on welfare for year after year when those people, with help and with assistance, could work, and so we're producing a much better system where we really put people through their paces and say that if you can work, you should work."[45]

"Large numbers are being checked... More than 70% [of people who were receiving Incapacity Benefit] who once would have languished unseen on a sickness benefit, will now be engaged on a journey to independence through work."[46]

These quotes imply two things. One is that people on Incapacity Benefit or Employment and Support Allowance are being or have been forgotten, 'languishing unseen.' The other is that these people are capable of work; their illness or disability is not so great as to prevent them from being able to work.

Languishing Unseen?

There is little evidence that people are 'festering' on benefits. The combined ESA and Incapacity Benefit (IB) caseload has been falling since 2004 (ESA was brought in to replace IB in 2008). There was an increase in caseload between the latter half of 2008 and 2009, but since then the caseload has been falling again.[47] This means that more people are leaving ESA and IB than are joining ESA.

More than half of ESA claims last less than 6 months, and 7 in 10 last less than one year. This is probably from a combination of people recovering enough to come off ESA

---

[44] Iain Duncan Smith, 27th June 2012, Speech on welfare to the Ways and Means Committee, House of Congress
[45] David Cameron, as quoted in Wintour, 26th July 2011, Employment benefit test finds two-thirds of claimants fit for work
[46] Iain Duncan Smith, 27th June 2012, Speech on welfare to the Ways and Means Committee, House of Congress
[47] data sourced from the DWP tabulation tool

and people who were originally deemed likely to recover being sent for a reassessment. In either case, the majority of recipients are not given long-term benefits, i.e. they have not been 'forgotten.' For those that have been given long claims, it is likely to be because they were correctly recognised as too ill or disabled to work.

Iain Duncan Smith has said that people on IB for more than two years are more likely to die or retire than get a job.[48] He cites this as a tragedy, but neglects to consider that people who have been chronically ill or disabled for two years are inherently more likely to have a condition that will impede their work ability for yet more years. It is simply the way a sickness benefit works: the more ill or disabled you are, the more likely you are to need benefits for a long period of time.

It is sensible to recognise that if a person has a permanent condition, there is unlikely to be a change in his or her need of benefits. When the US tried toughening its assessment criteria, it found that people moved off the benefit initially but within a few years were again on incapacity benefits; this may well be because their health was not good enough for sustained work.[49]

Independence Through Work?

Twelve to eighteen months after people were found 'fit for work' when making a new claim for ESA, 10% had gone back to the job they used to have, 18% had found a new job or become self-employed, and most (48%) went on another benefit; others appealed, retired, or did not claim any new benefit. Self-employment is not a secure income for the majority of people, and may only have been taken up because a person was too ill to be employable. Depending on the nature of the work, it has the benefit of being highly flexible to fit around an individual's health. These figures show that the majority found 'fit for work' do not, and may not be able to, return to work.

---

[48] BBC 27th May 2010 Welfare 'trapping' people in poverty says Iain Duncan Smith

[49] OECD, Transforming Disability into Ability, 2003

The figures refer to new claims, meaning that they are drawn from people who may be unsure of their qualification status and may also recover within 6 months. Reassessments from Incapacity Benefit are likely to have more difficulty in returning to work, because the fact they have been on support since at least 2008 means they have a long-term condition and have been away from the job market for several years.

The Responsible Reform report states that, "It was almost unanimously felt the Government has an overly optimistic view of life for disabled people in the United Kingdom today... Despite the Disability Discrimination Act 1995 and Equality 2010, many buildings remain inaccessible and most public transport, especially in rural areas, is similarly inaccessible or unreliable."[50] It remains more difficult for a disabled person to get a job; a non-disabled person with five A*-C GCSEs is more likely to be in employment than a disabled person with a university degree.[51] The barriers faced by disabled people have not reduced enough for the permanently disabled to now be able to access all parts of society.

Iain Duncan Smith's conclusion that "70% who once would have languished unseen on a sickness benefit, will now be engaged on a journey to independence through work," has no empirical support. Unless and until the government focuses on the support, adaptations and flexible working practices necessary for chronically ill and disabled people to be able to work, the re-assessment of people with long-term conditions is unlikely to have much beneficial effect on the people concerned.

Work is Good For You?

"For too long in this country we have left people on welfare for year after year when those people, with help and with assistance, could work, and so we're producing a much better system where we really put people through their paces and say

---

[50] Campbell, Marsh, Franklin, Gaffney, Dixon, James, Barnett-Cormack, Fon-James, Willis, et al 2012 Responsible

[51] Aldridge, Parekh, MacInnes and Kenway 2011, Monitoring Poverty and Social Exclusion, JRF

that if you can work, you should work... That will be good for them, good for their families and good for our economy."[52]

The government is very keen to get people (back) into work. In particular they are targeting those who have been on long-term benefits, including the disabled who have been 'abandoned' to 'fester.' Organisations representing disabled people agree that many disabled people want to work and are capable of work. What these organisations tend to focus on is the changes to working practice, technological adaptations and other support that will enable people with disabilities to work. What the government seems to be talking about is getting people off benefits without creating a society that enables work for currently disabled people.

There is also little evidence that people are being left on welfare 'for year after year,' as the above section explained.

There is general consensus that work, on average, brings health benefits. Returning to work is associated with rises in self-esteem, general health and mental health, with falls in psychological distress and minor psychiatric morbidity. Unemployment is linked with poor health; however this is due largely not to lack of structure or meaningful work, but rather to the financial uncertainty and poverty that is associated with unemployment.[53]

There are multiple provisos to the statement that work brings health benefits. Work that is monotonous or repetitive, lacks autonomy, has a poor balance between effort and reward or provides low financial security does not bring the positive effects that higher quality work would bring.[54] Furthermore, no long-term studies of the impact of work on the health of chronically ill people have been carried out. The government's report that briefly considered this concluded that there is a significant minority for whom work has negative effects on health.[55]

---

[52] David Cameron, as quoted in Wintour, 26th July 2011, Employment benefit test finds two-thirds of claimants fit for work

[53] Waddell, 2006, Is work good for your health and well-being? DWP

[54] ibid.

[55] ibid. This study suggested this minority might be 5-10%

The government therefore needs to be very careful with its focus on 'work.' It needs to be aware that there are people who are incapable of work, and people for whom work would cause a deterioration in their health. For disabled and chronically ill people who can work, the government needs to put in place the provisions necessary for that work to be possible.

Fraud?

"But I hope, for the sake of the disabled, that Iain Duncan Smith won't give way when faced with wheelchairs chained to his railings: a system that allows fraud ultimately fails those with real disabilities."[56]

A system that allows high fraud is one that is failing. In any test, an assessment of the test's accuracy requires an understanding of both the false positive and the false negative rate. In the case of assessments of disability, this means looking at both the number of people who receive benefit when they shouldn't (fraud and over-payment) and the number of people who are denied benefit when they should be awarded it. Increasing the accuracy of one side (e.g., reducing fraud) risks decreasing accuracy at the other (i.e., denying money to those who need it).

No test is perfect – there will be people paid more money than they need, and there will be people paid less. The measure of whether or not the test fails depends on what you think is the correct balance between two factors – ensuring that no-one receives support who does not fully need it, or ensuring that no-one who needs support is denied it. Currently, high rejection rates, high appeal rates, high overturn rates at appeal and low fraud suggest that the current system is weighted towards reducing fraud.

Unfortunately, the facts regarding fraud (i.e. that fraud is low) are not reflected in the media or in public opinion. "Negative images of welfare claimants survived into the era of the modern welfare state, where the need to protect the vulnerable and to protect the interests of the taxpayer

---

[56] Christina Odone, 12th May 2012, Iain Duncan Smith must not give in to the 'disability bullies.' The Telegraph.

have become conflated in media and policy."[57] There has been an increase in "tabloid articles presenting the incapacity claimant as 'undeserving,'" and in those "focussing on incapacity benefit 'fraud' and using pejorative language such as 'cheats.'"[58]

Robert Winnett, writing in the Daily Telegraph, refers to "the experiences of tackling the abuse of incapacity benefit,"[59] as if abuse has been a high percentage of Incapacity Benefit payments. Tom Newton Dunn, in the Sun, refers to "MoD bureaucrats" as "insisting that wounded heroes get the same grilling as suspected cheats and scroungers,"[60] again as though many claimants are cheats and scroungers.[61]

A survey by the National Centre for Social Research in 2010 found that 84% of respondents agreed strongly or slightly that a large number or people falsely claim benefits.[62] The latest British Social Attitudes survey found that 35% of people agree with the statement "Most people on the dole are fiddling in one way or another."[63] A more detailed analysis in 2007 had found that 25% of the public considered more than half of all sickness and disability claims are false, whilst a further 45% considered between 1 in 5 and 1 in 2 claims to be false. 2.6% of people thought that false claims were 1 in 100 or fewer.[64] Given that this is the public understanding of the benefits system, it is

---

[57] David M Turner, February 2012, 'Fraudulent' disability in historical perspective, History and Policy

[58] Briant, Watson, Philo, 19th October 2011, Bad News for Disabled People, Inclusion London.

[59] Robert Winnett, 13th May 2012, Iain Duncan Smith: 'I'm not scared to light the fuse on disability reform.' The Telegraph.

[60] Tom Newton Dunn, 17th May 2012, Wounded Heroes Beat MoD in Benefits Battle, The Sun.

[61] Incidentally, the veterans 'won': they will not be subject to the same benefits test as the general public.

[62] 2011 British Social Attitudes: the 28th Report, London, NatCen Social Research.

[63] Park, Clery, Curtice, Phillips, and Utting,(eds.) 2012 British Social Attitudes: the 29th Report, London: NatCen Social Research

[64] 2007 British Social Attitudes: the 23rd Report, London, NatCen Social Research

understandable that there is general support for a reduction in the welfare bill and more effort to reduce false claims.

Compounding the messages given by the media and government is the hidden nature of many disabilities. In his article in the Telegraph, Robert Winnett goes on to say, "It is alleged that many people, who the public would not regard as disabled, can claim the allowance." But the public are not the judge of who is and is not disabled. As these stories show, there are many people who are not overtly disabled who still face massive and expensive barriers to work and life. What the public thinks is not relevant to whether or not a person is disabled.

All of this is contrary to reality. For disability or sickness-related claims, the reality is that only 1 in 200 claims for Disability Living Allowance are false. Fraud rates for Incapacity Benefit are even lower at 1 in 300.[65] In terms of cost, this amounts to £60 million for DLA and £10 million for IB. Both of these benefits lose more to errors made by customers (0.6 and 0.9% respectively) and errors by officials (0.8 and 1.2%) than to fraud. DLA is also underpaid by 2.4% due to customer error, and IB is underpaid by 0.7% due to official error. The evidence is that this is not a system rife with fraud.

At the other end, false negatives for these benefits are high. In some counties, over 90% of claimants originally turned down for ESA get the decision overturned in their favour. Many people simply reapply, rather than appeal, or give up, so the full count of incorrect refusals is even higher.

Christina Odone said that, "a system that allows fraud ultimately fails those with real disabilities." [66] This is a valid argument when a system pays so much on fraudulent claims that there isn't enough money to give

---

[65] Fraud and error in the benefit system, June 2012, DWP http://statistics.dwp.gov.uk/asd/asd2/fem/fem_preliminary_1112_revised.pdf

[66] Christina Odone, 12th May 2012, Iain Duncan Smith must not give in to the 'disability bullies.' The Telegraph.

genuine claims the support they need. The current system is different: it is one where there is so much emphasis on preventing fraud that genuine claims are turned away. The current system does not fail the disabled community by remaining pervious to a little fraud, it fails the disabled community by being so focussed on rooting out any fraud that it turns away genuine claims.

3

Who Cares? ESA and the Work Capability Assessment

The general public, some of whom may not have given much thought to the matter, might assume that the welfare state provides them with a safety net: that if they become ill and so lose employment they will be able to receive state support, and that this support is sufficient to meet minimum needs.

If so, the general public would be wrong.

This section focuses primarily on the Work Capability Assessment, which is used to assess a sick person's capability for work. It looks at how well this system works and how the assessment for ESA is made. It also briefly considers the extent to which payments, when they are made, are adequate to meet the recipient's needs.

What is ESA?

Employment and Support Allowance (ESA) is the successor to Incapacity Benefit. It was designed under Labour, and brought into use nationally by the Coalition. Before it was rolled out nationwide, some of the key designers warned that it was not fit for nationwide use. It has attracted a lot of controversy and has been the subject of two television documentaries by Panorama and Dispatches.

ESA is paid on either a means-tested or contributions-based basis.

Support for those who are considered capable of 'work-related activity', and who have paid National Insurance contributions, is limited to one year. It is not dependent on how much has been paid in National Insurance contributions, but instead depends simply on whether a person has spent the majority of the last three years in work or not. The House of Lords voted in a recommendation that the support be extended from one to two years, but this was over-turned in the House of Commons. Young people, who have not had the chance to work for three years because they have been in education, will not get contribution-based support.

If help is still needed after the one-year time limit on contribution based support, it is provided on a means-tested basis. Anyone whose partner earns above £7500 a year gets no help. This leaves many people in poverty. According to the Joseph Rowntree Foundation, pensioners are the only group of people for whom means-tested benefits are sufficient to achieve a decent living standard.[67] For everyone else, means-tested benefits are not adequate.

With the changes in the benefits system, to be brought in in 2013, ESA will come under Universal Credit (UC) – but only if it is paid as income-based (means-tested) ESA. Universal Credit is a new benefit that will replace child tax credit, working tax credit, housing benefit, income based employment and support allowance, income based jobseekers allowance, income support and parts of the social fund. Contribution-based ESA will be paid separately. The assessment process will remain the same as it currently is.

A person may be found

- fit for work
- unfit for work but fit for work-related activity, or
- unfit for work-related activity.

Claimants found fit for work will be put onto Jobseeker's Allowance and expected to carry out the various activities that are mandatory for Jobseekers in order to continue receiving the benefit. Those in the second category are assigned to the Work-related Activity Group. Continuing receipt of ESA is dependent on attendance at interviews with a member of Jobcentre staff and at various

---

[67] Aldridge, Parekh, MacInnes and Kenway, 2011, Monitoring Povery and Social Exclusion, JRF

training sessions. Claimants in the third category go into the Support Group; no demands are made of them.

An ESA assessment starts with a request for ESA. The claimant is then sent a questionnaire to complete. A decision may be made just on this questionnaire, but this is rare. Most often a person is asked to attend a Work Capability Assessment. In the meantime, payment is made at the same rate as Jobseeker's Allowance, which is lower than the rate for ESA.

The questionnaire starts with basic information, including any help needed during the assessment, such as difficulty with using stairs or public transport, or needing a British Sign Language signer. There is space to describe your illness, disability or condition and how it affects you, including any aids that are used. This is an important space, particularly for those with fluctuating conditions, to explain exactly what impact their condition has. This is followed with questions about medical treatment.

The next section deals with physical functions. It asks about the distance and manner of walking, any pain or discomfort or any aids that are used. Then there is a question on steps – whether or not you can walk up or down two steps without help from another person.[68] The next question is about the ability to move from one seat to an adjacent seat and the ability to remain in one place, either standing or sitting, and includes changes in position without needing the aid of another person.

Some of these questions seem to have set the bar very high. Many claimants may have pain and exhaustion which make such movements difficult, yet would respond to these questions in the affirmative. In particular, asking about a mere two steps gives the suggestion that the interest is in the binary distinction of being able to use a step or not. By not giving a few points for difficulty using more than two steps it becomes impossible to assess the cumulative effect of being moderately limited in use of steps and in other areas.

---

[68] It is worth noting that this is a drastic change from the precursor to the Work Capability Assessment, where 15 steps were considered.

After this comes a question on reaching, which focusses on the ability to lift one arm high enough to reach a top pocket in a coat or jacket, and the ability to lift one arm above head height. Then there is a question about picking things up with one arm: specifically, 500 ml or 1 pint of liquid, 1000 ml or 2 pints of liquid, and a large, empty cardboard box. Again these seem to be very high standards. A person may be able to lift one arm a few times, but what if having done so they have no strength to grip or hold? What then is the use of being able to lift one arm? What relation does this have to any type of work?

Having established the ability to carry small *or* light objects, then comes a question on manual dexterity (note that by the nature of the questions a person may be unable to carry a large item of noticeable weight, yet still pass this section). This question covers the ability to use one hand to press a button, turn the pages of a book, pick up a £1 coin, use a pen or pencil, use a computer keyboard and use a computer mouse. Repetition is not asked about, and again there is no option to consider the cumulative effect of multiple minor difficulties, which may overall be worse than one major difficulty.

The next couple of questions look at communication, focussing on physical rather than mental difficulties at this stage. The questions ask whether or not you can communicate through speech or the written word without the help of another person. They do not ask how difficult this may be, how long it takes, what compensations have to be made, or how heavily your ability is reliant on skills or technology possessed by other people.

Visual problems are specifically focussed on in the next question in relation to the ability to get around. This is different from any other physical difficulty with movement, as it is about the ability to see and how this affects ability to move safely. The question is specifically about the ability to get around without assistance from another person. Again, there is no concern about the level of difficulty or speed in getting around alone, as long as one can get around alone.

The next question is particularly personal, and can be distressing for claimants to fill out. It deals with the ability to control their bladder and bowels, including using a collecting device such as a stoma and bag. This question completes the section on physical functions.

The second section is on mental, cognitive and intellectual functions. It asks about difficulty with learning new tasks, awareness of hazards or danger during the execution of everyday tasks, and the ability to plan, start and finish daily tasks. Whilst difficulties with learning new tasks can clearly be seen as relevant to the workplace, it is more difficult to see how asking about everyday and daily tasks gives any insight into a person's ability to carry out work-related tasks. Such tasks may well be more complicated, contain a greater number of steps, and involve less familiar actions.

This is followed up with a question about the ability to cope with small changes to routine, either with or without warning. However many jobs may involve large changes in routine, or indeed a lack of any set routine in a way that is relevant to this question.

Having already asked about physical difficulties with getting around, this questionnaire now asks about the mental side of going out. It specifically asks about the ability to go out alone; however it gives only a yes or no option to this, without the option for people who may sometimes be able to go out alone, but not every time or reliably. Whilst there were questions about the ability to get around in terms of physical difficulties, there was no question that specifically asked whether the person *for physical reasons* needs another person in order to get around outdoors, e.g. to push a wheelchair.

The questionnaire finishes with a couple of questions about social situations. The first asks about the ability to meet people, either known or not, without feeling anxious or scared. The second asks about the ability to behave in a way that does not upset other people. Disappointingly, there are no questions on how mental, cognitive or intellectual conditions affect the ability to communicate.

Most of the questions give, where relevant, the option to select yes, no, or it varies, or some sort of scale from daily to occasionally, again usually with an 'it varies' option. The questions also have text boxes so that more information can be given.

The information from the Work Capability Assessment, with the questionnaire and any supporting evidence from a claimant's doctor(s), are then sent to a DWP decision maker. The decision maker uses this evidence to decide whether or not to award ESA, and if so which group to put the claimant in (Work-related activity group or Support group).

The overall Work Capability Assessment is considered by many in the disabled community to be flawed, inaccurate and unfit for use. It is one of the harshest, if not the harshest, such assessment in the developed world.[69] Since being rolled out nation-wide the assessment for ESA has found a high percentage of applicants as 'fit for work' who are demonstrably not capable of work, sometimes with tragic consequences.

Who is responsible for its effectiveness?

Disability rights groups have laid much stress on the role of Atos, the company contracted by the DWP to carry out WCAs. Protests have been held outside Atos buildings, and online groups have been set up to share stories of WCA experiences. The General Medical Council is currently investigating doctors and nurses for poor conduct. Professor Harrington, in charge of conducting three independent reviews of the ESA system, said in his second review that, "The onus for the delivery of sound, accurate and effective assessments… rests heavily on Atos."

But Atos did not design the WCA or set the rules. These roles belong to the government, and changing the provider of WCAs may have no effect on the accuracy or equity of

[69] Organisation for Economic Co-operation and Development, 2003, Transforming disability into ability, policies to promote work and income security for disabled people.

the WCAs. A spokesperson for Atos said, "Our trained doctors, nurses and physiotherapists use their clinical knowledge and apply the Government's policy and criteria to each assessment."[70] Another spokesperson said, "We carry out all assessments within the criteria and policy guidelines set by the Government."[71] Whilst it is difficult to assign culpability when the government refuses to publish details of the contract with Atos, the government as the employer bears final responsibility and is therefore the one to be considered ultimately culpable in this matter. Atos should not be pilloried for carrying out work as asked by the government.

Who carries out the assessment?

Work Capability Assessments for Employment and Support Allowance are made by the company Atos Healthcare. Atos is a multi-national IT company, and Atos Healthcare employs doctors, nurses and physiotherapists to assess, in 45 minutes, what a claimant is capable of doing. A Freedom of Information request made in November 2011 revealed that just over half of Atos health care professionals (HCPs) were doctors, the rest were nurses or physiotherapists. However, in terms of full-time equivalents (ignoring sessional workers, for which no information is held), nurses and physiotherapists made up over 70% of the workforce.

Dr Margaret McCartney wrote to the British Medical Journal to question the ethics of allowing those without specialist knowledge to carry out assessments.[72] She says that, "Training is provided for each type of benefit examination. Its length... depends on experience but is generally up to five days of classroom training, followed by sessions accompanied by a trainer that are audited

[70] Greenaway, 24th September 2012, Nurse makes heartfelt apology after Atos forced her to trick disabled people out of benefits. Daily Record.

[71] Phillips, 27th September 2012, Denied disability benefits after a lifetime of hard work. Mirror.

[72] McCartney, Well Enough to Work? 2011 British Medical Journal; 342:d599

afterwards."[1] She does not seem to consider this to be adequate. It takes many years for a doctor to become a consultant; no assessor can have consultant-level knowledge of every condition. Can a person with sub-specialist knowledge accurately examine the veracity of a claimant's claims or understand the debilitating nature of his or her condition? A system that allowed less-specialised health care professionals to handle the relatively simple cases, whilst passing on those with rare, severe, complex or multiple conditions to specialists, might provide more accurate assessments.

However, Professor Harrington, commissioned by the government to carry out three independent reviews, spoke of their training as having impressive scope and depth. According to a Freedom of Information request, and as also said by Professor Harrington, these focus largely on disability assessment medicine and using tools such as LiMA. It is therefore difficult to make a judgement on an Atos HCPs' knowledge of many conditions, and whether or not this knowledge has the depth necessary to make an informed assessment of any given condition.

There is some recognition by Atos that not all health professionals have sufficiently extensive knowledge to be able to assess a claimant accurately – only doctors may assess claimants with neurological conditions. However, conditions such as Myalgic Encephalomyelitis, recognised as neurological by the World Health Organisation and the UK, do not have to be assessed by a doctor.

The health care professional does not have access to the claimant's medical notes and has no prior knowledge of the claimant and the detail of his or her conditions. Thus they lack insight into the claimant's specific experience of his or her condition(s), what treatments have been tried, and what has or has not been successful in helping manage the condition. Nor do they know the nuances of the claimant's health. Another person with the same illness will have a different combination of symptoms and symptom severity, which means he or she is capable of things that the first person cannot do, and vice versa. 66% of ESA claimants have more than one condition.[73]

Recruitment fairs for Atos stress the 9-5 hours of this job. Dr McCartney reports, "The message from the recruitment evening was quite clear. We were told, 'You are not in a typical caring role. This isn't about diagnosing,' and 'We (Atos) don't call them patients . . . We call them claimants.'" The implication is that there is more focus on the working hours than on care for the person being assessed. Of course, this is a generalisation; some people have reported having assessors with very friendly personas, but many people report a lack of sympathy or care.

An open letter to the British Medical Journal and Royal College of Nurses expands on this. The authors write, "Doctors' and nurses' ethics are being corrupted by Atos' offers of higher salaries and daytime reduced work hours. Some doctors have tried to argue that their duty to claimants does not apply when assessing benefit patients on behalf of Atos. But the General Medical Council has upheld that doctors are always bound by this duty whether seeing patients, employees (when assessing occupational health), benefit and insurance claimants, and athletes, among others... Claimants rightly fear that most Atos assessors are uncaring and prejudiced – they work to targets which have nothing to do with patients' individual health needs or with the realities of the job market which sick and disabled people are being thrown into."[74]

Shortcomings in the Work Capability Assessment (LiMA and the HCP)

Atos won the contract to carry out WCAs on the basis of their computer program, LiMA. LiMA is a series of drop-down boxes which the assessor selects on the basis of comments made by the claimant. After recommendations made by Professor Harrington, Health Care Professionals

[73] Sissons, Barnes and Stevens. 2011 Routes onto ESA. DWP

[74] http://benefitclaimantsfightback.wordpress.com/open-letter-on-atos-healthcare-to-the-bmj-and-rcn/ One of many sites on which this open letter can be read.

are now encouraged to use the free text boxes to ensure that the report is individualised. The technical manual for LiMA stresses that responsibility lies with the HCP, and that LiMA should not be used in a way that overrides the clinical judgement of the HCP.[75]

The computer takes the selected words to generate sentences, although these sentences may not otherwise relate to statements made by the claimant. Several statements are frequently cited on Internet sites as evidence of the failings of the WCA.[76] However, these largely relate to the Personal Capability Assessment for Incapacity Benefit. As changes have been made to LiMA and the use of it by HCPs since then, these statements should not continue to be propagated as having any bearing on the ESA assessment process. Claimants have however been told more recently, "I believe you aren't capable of work, but I can't make you fit the criteria,"[77] demonstrating the continued inability of the system to cope with the complexities of reality.

LiMA uses earlier selections to prompt later questions and selections. This has the adverse effect that any early errors are propagated throughout the report. If the HCP relies too heavily on the prompting, important relevant information may not be included. As an example, neck pain may not be used by LiMA as a factor in ability to sit, even though it can cause great difficulties.[78]

LiMA is programmed to give more weight to observed behaviour than to either the history or the examination;[79] yet so much of an illness is hidden. You could look at me and not know if I have any of a huge range of medical conditions. I might have holes in my back draining my kidneys into a bag. I could have epileptic fits several times

[75] LiMA WCA Review Exam Application Technical Guide June 2011.

[76] See Appendix 2.

[77] Dryburgh and Lancashire, The Work Capability Assessment, 2010, Citizen's Advice Scotland

[78] This occurred under IB. The claimant was incorrectly found fit for work, because the neck pain was not taken into account. CIB/476/2005 There may be other situations in which similar problems occur.

[79] LiMA WCA Review Exam Application Technical Guide June 2011

a week. I might be in huge amounts of pain and be extremely sensitive to touch. I could hear voices or be suicidal. I may forget anything that has happened more than a few hours ago. One ill woman was assessed as fit to work because she "did not appear to be trembling... sweating... or make rocking movements". This was despite "two GPs, a psychiatrist and a senior nurse stating that she is not able to work or seek work."[80] An assessor may see a person come in, and conclude that the claimant is able to get around on the basis that the claimant made it to the assessment centre; yet there is no observable evidence of the pain, fatigue, cost or trauma this may have involved. People have been assessed as able to hear their name called, despite being deaf and relying either on lip-reading or an assistant.

The questions asked by the HCP do not always bear much relevance to the workplace or to the claimant's condition. Claimants and Citizen's Advice Bureaux (CAB) advisers have complained that questions are too narrow and limited. This leads to people who are incapable of work being found fit for work. The CAB continues to hear reports of "rushed assessments, assumptions being made without exploration, inaccurate recording and poor recognition of mental health problems."[81]

Claimants report frustration on the part of the assessor when a simple 'yes/no' answer is not given.[82] Such close-ended questions are a classic debating technique, to force the respondent to say something other than their original intention and to close off the option of giving further detail. The assessor may ask "Do you do your own laundry?" or "Do you prepare a main meal?" These questions have yes/no answers. They have no room for explaining how difficult these tasks are. It means that people who do these tasks out of necessity, because there is no-one else to do them, are penalised. This is despite the

---

[80] New benefit will fail to spot illness and disability, 2010, Mind
[81] Royston, Not Working, March 2010, Citizen's Advice Bureau www.citizensadvice.org.uk/not_working
[82] Dryburch and Lancashire, The Work Capability Assessment, 2010, Citizen's Advice Scotland

fact that the very completion of these tasks may render any other activity, whether work-related or not, even more difficult.

Compounding this difficulty is the sideways manner in which assessors ask questions. Rather than ask, 'for how long are you able to concentrate?' the question is 'Do you watch any TV?' If the answer is 'Yes, I watch such and such a program' then the claimant is assessed as being able to concentrate and sit in a chair for the length of the given program. Yet those were not the questions asked.

As an example, it is worth considering to what extent 'watching TV' equates to 'able to sit easily for prolonged periods of time.' The chair may well be one specially adapted for the user to ensure comfort. Even if not, resting in a comfortable armchair is rarely equivalent to sitting upright in an office chair, however well-adapted. Nor is the question 'how often do you have to change position?' asked. The claimant may stand up for a few minutes to relieve pain, or watch television lying down. Employers may not be able to make a workstation fit a person lying down, or would be happy for half the time at work to be spent in moving around, trying to find a more comfortable position or relieve pain.

The issue of concentration is even bigger. Is watching half an hour of a soap opera really equivalent to half an hour of work? If that were the case, TVs would be a lot less common. Watching TV is something most of us categorise as 'relaxing'. It is what we do to rest after work. For a person with chronic health problems, TV is often a distraction, an attempt to give one's mind something other than illness to think about. It also relieves loneliness, albeit not very well, creating an artificial sense of companionship and contact with other people.

Yet more dangerous than this assumption that watching TV is a mental challenge for a healthy person is the assumption that 'I watch such and such a program,' means 'I am fully able to concentrate, comprehend and critically think for 30-60 minutes, and thus am able to work for 8 hours a day, 5 days a week, 47 weeks a year.' Two fallacies are being committed. One, the most obvious, is that 30-60 minutes a day is not equivalent to 8 hours. It's like saying, "You can run one to three miles. Therefore you can run a marathon." The other fallacy is the assumption that the claimant is concentrating, comprehending and critically thinking for thirty minutes. The claimant has not been asked 'how long can you concentrate?' and therefore has not answered this question. It is very possible that the claimant 'watches' TV in the sense of 'It is on, I am in the same room, I vaguely look towards it, and I am not doing anything else.' This is so far from sustained work that the comparison makes a mockery of the assessment. Asking questions about TV will not get a response that contains reliable information about ability to work.

There are many other situations in which an answer to one question is used as a reply to a more demanding query that has not been asked. It is common for claimants to be assessed as able to walk 200m on the flimsiest of evidence. The evidence, perhaps, was that the claimant 'appeared' to walk without difficulty from the waiting area to the consulting room. Yet appearances are deceiving. If you, as an adult, have not yet learnt this, then there are serious questions about your ability to assess the health of another person.

The DWP instructed its medical assessors to, "Bear in mind that a person who can easily manage around the house and garden is unlikely to be limited to walking less than 200 metres; a person who can walk around a shopping centre/supermarket is unlikely to be limited to walking less than 800 metres."[83] I have not found any evidence to support this. And who decides what is 'easily manage'? To walk from one room to another in a house would rarely be above a 10 metre walk (unless it included stairs, but we're not talking about an ability to use stairs here). And people don't tend to walk back and forth between any two rooms 20 times for the fun of it, or to and from the garden and the nearest room. There is no logical reason to extrapolate the ability to move around a house and garden to being able to walk 200m.

---

[83] ESA Handbook for Approved Doctors, DWP; as quoted in Not Working, 2010, CAB

At times it feels as though the DWP, decision makers and HCPs are speaking a different language to the person being assessed. When I say I can 'manage' around the house and garden, what I mean is: I rarely, if ever, move above 10 metres at a time and certainly not as much as 20m; I move from one sitting position to another; I am willing to move because there are walls and furniture to lean on and if I fall at least it is indoors; the floor is largely polished wood so shuffling meets little resistance. I certainly do not mean that I can walk 200m, because the reality is that I cannot walk that far; however in DWP language that is exactly what I am taken to mean.

As for 800m around a supermarket, consider this case: "A client was asked if she ever went to the supermarket. She responded that she did sometimes go with her husband if it was a good day, but was not allowed to explain more than this. She explained to the bureau that it was a very small supermarket and she only went up a couple of short aisles. She was staggered when she saw her WCA report and found that the HCP had used this as evidence that she could walk 800 metres."[84] It is an important part of the ESA assessment process that a claimant be able to carry out an action reliably, as well as repeatedly and safely, so in this case the assessor failed to carry out the assessment correctly. Because this claimant was not allowed to explain how often good days occurred, how often on a good day she could go around the supermarket, how well she would cope (if at all) if her husband were not present to help keep her safe, or what happens on a bad day, an incorrect assessment of her ability was made. This ability to walk, on a good day and with her husband, up two short aisles does not equate to an ability to walk 800m reliably, repeatedly or safely; it therefore should not be used as evidence for such.

The DWP went on to say, "Consider basic functions of personal care such as brushing teeth. This would involve remembering to put toothpaste onto a brush and brushing all areas of teeth. This may be regarded as a simple task. Other aspects of personal care may be the ability to be able

---

[84] Royston, Not Working, March 2010, Citizen's Advice Bureau

to get up, showered, shave, clean teeth, select clothing items and get dressed appropriately for the weather outside. *This may represent an ability to understand and retain information.*"[85]

This cannot be a reliable conclusion. Some actions that we learn and use repeatedly become habitual and require little conscious effort to retain. Actions such as walking, cycling, changing gear whilst driving, playing an often-practised piece of music and knowing the correct procedure for brushing one's teeth become almost instinctive. This is not an indicator of the ability to understand and retain information, as this case highlights: "A bureau adviser in Yorkshire was surprised to find that a client who attended a special school, who could not read or write and who clearly found it difficult to grasp instructions, was awarded no points under the descriptors intended to cover those with learning difficulties."[86]

The WCA does not ask questions that are relevant to the work place, so will not elicit responses that give reliable answers to such work-related questions.

Are the ESA descriptors fit for purpose?

There has also been concern that the descriptors against which a person is measured are too narrow.[87]

RSI action, in a memorandum to the DWP on the ESA descriptors, said, "Some of the WCA descriptors have no relevance to the workplace. For example descriptor 5C (cannot pick up and move light bulky objects such as a cardboard box, requiring the use of both hands together) is not relevant to the workplace. During the DWP review of the WCA in March this year, a medical adviser to the DWP claimed that this descriptor described the requirements for a shelf stacker in Sainsbury's, moving goods from a trolley onto the shelf. However the descriptor is for moving from one side to another a large but light object, such as an

[85] ESA Handbook for Approved Doctors, DWP; as quoted in Not Working, 2010, CAB; my emphasis added
[86] Royston, Not Working, March 2010, Citizen's Advice Bureau
[87] A guide to ESA – the WCA, June 2011, DWP

empty cardboard box. Such a claim is unsupportable: supermarkets do not sell empty cardboard boxes, and most goods are of a significant weight (single jars or cans 400g upwards, bottle of coke 2kg, bottle of wine 1.3kg, can of beer 475g). Multiple packs of 4x, 6x or 24x multiply the individual weight of such a retail item to between 4 and 10 kg. Even in an office environment objects have real weight (the governments Green Paper on Shaping the Future of Care Together weighs 485g, a ream of office paper weighs 2.3kg), and office workers (particularly low paid workers) are often expected to move multiple items as part of their normal work…

The ESA50 gives no guidance to the benefit applicant that the WCA assessment is to consider activities in a work setting, where activities would be expected to be undertaken reliably, repeatedly and safely. That is to say to be undertaken on a bad day as well as a good day, to be repeated a number of times as part of the working day, and to be undertaken safely without injury, pain or further injury. For example, the fact that an applicant can fill in a form over a number of hours or days, does not constitute an ability to write within a working environment."[88]

The descriptors[89] are similar to the questions asked in the questionnaire, so have the problems discussed earlier. For example, the inability to use a pen or pencil to make a meaningful mark seems to be set at a very high standard; this may mean that anyone who can make a mark in a tick-box or sign their name as an X is considered not to be limited in their ability to write, even if they are unable to write – because of arthritis for example. Or if a claimant has the ability to convey a simple message to strangers, such as the presence of a hazard, this may be construed as the ability to communicate in a work setting, where messages may well be complex. The ability to *understand* a simple message is examined only in relation to sensory impairments, rather than any fatigue, mental health condition or learning difficulty. Overall the barriers seem

[88] Decision making and appeals in the benefits system, 2010; Memorandum submitted by RSI Action
[89] A guide to ESA – the WCA, June 2011, DWP

to have been set so high that one wonders whether anyone designed them with any relation to any workplace.

The assessment process – a challenge in itself

The assessment process can be difficult and traumatic. For people with mental health issues it can exacerbate their condition.[90] For many claimants, it is physically impossible to turn up to an appointment unassisted, and very difficult even with assistance. The process can cause physical pain and severe mental distress. For sufferers and their carers, Atos is "feared and loathed probably in equal terms."[91]

There are 139 assessment centres in the UK. A Freedom of Information request revealed that of these, 39 (28%) do not have wheelchair access, 86 do not have either on-site, opposite or next-door parking, and 60 are not accessible by public transport.[92] This means that there are a great many centres which are not accessible to the clientele, i.e. people with disabilities. These are extraordinary failures by Atos, and contravene the Disability Discrimination Act and the Equality Act. A senior representative of Atos admitted that appointments are routinely overbooked by 20%; Atos reports that a similar percentage fail to turn up for appointments, but this does not help those who are left waiting in uncomfortable circumstances.

Is decision-making fit for purpose?

The assessors employed by Atos are not the 'decision makers.' Decision Makers are workers at the Department of Work and Pensions, who are not medical professionals. They may not have the understanding necessary to make accurate decisions. For example, I have been prescribed diazepam, which many people do not recognise or understand. However if I say that I have been prescribed Valium, suddenly a lot more people have insight into one

---

90 Dryburgh and Lancashire, The Work Capability Assessment, 2010, Citizen's Advice Scotland

91 Liberal Democrat MP Stephen Lloyd

92 http://www.whatdotheyknow.com/request/atos_assessment_centres_location

of my health problems and what effect it may have on my life.

DWP workers are told to consider all medical evidence, yet "the Jobcentre Plus Decision Makers do not in practice make decisions, but instead they typically 'rubber stamp' the advice provided through the Atos assessment. They often do not have or do not appropriately consider additional evidence submitted to support a claim for [ESA]. This results in the Atos assessment driving the whole process, rather than being seen in its proper context as part of the process."[93] In parliamentary reports, there have been strong recommendations that the decision is not made just on the Atos report. Yet the House of Commons ruled against an amendment by the House of Lords to make it compulsory to submit medical evidence from a claimant's doctor. However, Professor Harrington has recommended that decision makers carry out more liaison with claimants and HCPs in making their decision, so it is to be hoped that this will improve the decision making process.

Professor Harrington has found that there is high variability between decision makers. He said that "consistency and quality of decision making appear to be key issues." This is particularly the case now that Harrington's recommendations have led to an increased importance of the decision maker's role, relative to the ATOS assessment. In the meantime, many claimants are suffering from the poor consistency and quality of decisions.

Not all countries make decisions the way we do. Some, such as Switzerland, ask a claimant's doctor to assess the claim for benefits. 12% of these assessments are then checked by a superintendent to ensure accuracy and consistency. Here they don't have to ask someone with no knowledge of a claimant to make a judgement in 45 minutes of that claimant's health and ability to work.

---

[93] Professor Malcolm Harrington, *An Independent Review of the Work Capability Assessment - year two*, November 2011. There has been a slight increase since this report in the percentage of DWP decisions that disagree with the WCA recommendation.

The social model: the real barrier to work

"The one thing I am absolutely, unreservedly and implacably opposed to in all of this is a real world test." - Chris Grayling, then Minister for Employment, Department for Work and Pensions, 2011.

The difference between social and medical models of disease is one reason for the failure of the methodology underpinning an assessment of ability to work. By ignoring the difficulties presented to disabled people by society, both the Work Capability Assessment and the assessment process proposed for PIP fail to recognise just how disabling disability can be. Consequently, they fail to make assessments that accurately reflect the extent of need or ability to work.

Professor Richard Berthoud, in a paper arguing for the introduction of a real-world test, said, "The concept of incapacity is strongly rooted in the medical (or personal) model of disability, in which it is assumed that individuals' impairments – their inability to undertake normal activities like walking or seeing – directly prevent them from getting to work or from undertaking the tasks that are valued by employers. The social model of disability argues that it is the failure of care provision, transport networks or employers to adapt to varying needs that excludes disabled people from the labour market."[94]

Talking about the importance of the social model, the Office for Disability Issues said, "The social model understands that it is these barriers to participation that have the disabling effects on the individual rather than the individual's impairments themselves. The social model is able to encompass physical, mental, sensory, cognitive and intellectual impairments. In contrast, a medical model understanding of disability considers that people's impairments have the disabling effect. It is generally accepted that the medical model is less able to encompass the full range of impairments and is more likely to focus on physical conditions. The Office for Disability Issues, the

---

[94] https://www.iser.essex.ac.uk/publications/working-papers/iser/2011-22.pdf

public body whose role is to promote disability equality across Government departments, fully endorses the social model and considers the medical model to be outdated."[95]

In commenting on the importance of the social model for Personal Independence Payments, where a social model is just as important as it is for ESA, Scope said, "This point was highlighted by a man who attended our public meeting in Neath Port Talbot. He was a wheelchair user who was fit enough to have recently completed a half-marathon. However, he faced the same barriers to using public transport, for example railway stations which are not fully wheelchair accessible, as less physically able wheelchair users. As a result he incurred the same extra costs using taxis. Eugene Grant of Scope was concerned that the draft criteria [for PIP] as set out indicated an "overarching principle" of defining ability rather than assessing barriers. He argued this would only give part of the picture, allowing assessors to only partly establish the barriers people faced.

A recent report on the Welfare Reform Bill by our colleagues on the Joint Committee on Human Rights concluded that an approach that took better account of the social, practical and environmental barriers disabled people face would be less likely to lead to incompatibilities with the UK's obligations under the UN Convention on the Rights of Persons with Disabilities."[96]

Comments from other individuals and organisations tell us that, "The DWP have no model of what work is in the 21st century, and what activities workers are expected to carry out, or how frequently these work activities would be repeated. Consequently there is no traceability between the WCA descriptors and work in the 21st century..."[97] "...And the system rests on a deeply flawed premise—that

---

[95] See The social model of disability: http://odi.dwp.gov.uk/about-the-odi/the-social-model.php

[96] Legislative Scrutiny: Welfare Reform Bill, Joint Committee on Human Rights, Twenty-first Report of Session 2010-12; HL Paper 233/HC 1704 para 1.75

[97] Decision making and appeals in the benefits system, 2010; Memorandum submitted by RSI Action

there is a way to objectively determine who is able to work and who is not."[98]

And to conclude, "There is strong evidence that the system can be impersonal and mechanistic, that the process lacks transparency and that a lack of communication between the various parties involved contributes to poor decision making and a high rate of appeals," and that "evidence has consistently and regularly highlighted problems with each stage of the WCA process, which limit both the assessment's fairness and effectiveness."[99]

Is the assessment process accurate?

One illustration of the accuracy of the assessment is a comment made by Professor Paul Gregg before the WCA was rolled out nationally. He reported that, "the test so far has caused a huge amount of anguish to the people who have gone through it. We need to have something that is working accurately before we apply it nationally. We shouldn't roll this out until we have something that is working."[100] Gregg was involved in the design of the new system (ESA and WCA) and has been described as "one of the most rigorous and high-impact social policy academics in the UK."[101] The government did not follow the recommendation.

The assessment process is not reliably accurate. A recent CAB report found that of 37 assessments, *16* were substantially incorrect. These inaccuracies were omissions, incorrect recording of procedures (e.g. reporting that a claimant who could not sit easily could sit easily), incorrect

---

[98] http://www.guernicamag.com/features/kovich_9_15_11/ This quote refers to American Social Security. However, UK Social Security is also based on 'objective' measures, and the government's aim with PIP is to make the assessment process even more 'objective.'

[99] Professor Malcolm Harrington, An Independent Review of the Work Capability Assessment - year two, November 2011.

[100] Gentleman, 22nd Feb 2011, New disability test "is a complete mess," says expert, The Guardian.

[101] Baumberg, September 27th 2012, Paul Gregg: new ideas for disability, employment and welfare reform. Inequalities.

recording of the history given by the claimant (e.g. can dress unaided when the claimant can't do this), incorrect medical evidence (i.e. the assessor reports on something which the assessor is not in a position to accurately report on), information not being gathered (e.g. not allowing time to answer, or asking closed questions) and inconsistency within the report (one claimant was reported separately as having weekly and monthly hypo attacks; the latter was used – incorrectly – to determine points). Only 10 of the 37 had no or low levels of inaccuracy.

It is not uncommon for a claimant to be signed off work by a GP, and yet be refused benefits.[102] Nor is it unknown for an employer to consider an employee to be too ill to return to work, yet the employee is refused ESA.[103] The DWP argue that this is because the ESA assessment considers the ability to carry out any job, not just the one the claimant was in before becoming ill. However this still conflicts with the GP's judgement, and the questions asked are so poor that it is often unclear what job the DWP has in mind when assessing a person as fit for work.

Fit to work?

There needs to be more consideration of how a person may be able to work. A person who needs substantial special provisions may not be very employable. Nearby parking, lifts, specially adapted chairs and workstations, computer software adaptations - not all of these are available, nor can all companies afford to provide them. Unpredictable working is another major issue. A person's ability to work may change on an hourly, daily, weekly or monthly basis. This makes things very difficult for an employer who may have deadlines or need certain shifts covered. There are also likely to be issues with quality and errors, as so much of a disabled or chronically ill person's energy and brainpower is directed towards the more necessary business of managing their health problems.

---

[102] Dryburgh, Unfit for Purpose, 2010, Citizen's Advice Scotland.
[103] Dryburgh and Lancashire, The Work Capability Assessment, 2010, Citizen's Advice Scotland

Work is generally viewed as beneficial. At times this comes too close to an attitude that work is, unequivocally, in every situation, a complete blessing. This ignores a government report made in 2006 that beneficial effects of work and paid employment rely on a strong proviso of the quality of job and social context.[104] The beneficial effects of work occur in part through improved financial wealth and security, and improved mental health (e.g. because of raised self-esteem). Work that is poorly paid and/or demeaning is therefore unlikely to be "the best form of welfare."

There has been little study on the effects of work for those who are sick and disabled. It is likely that where studies show a positive effect, this is because those who are in work were already in a better state of health, and not because work led to an improvement in health. Indeed, if sick and disabled people return to work because of being disallowed benefits (suggesting financial stress, not health, is the reason of returning to work), most report that their health remains the same or deteriorates; this is also the case for those who appeal after being disallowed benefits. To assume that 'work is freeing' for the sick and disabled is a dangerous position to take.

In short, a person needs to be fit and well to be able to do a job well. Expecting an unwell person to work is likely to be counter-productive, and to have a damaging effect on the person's health; nor is it good for employers to have a less than healthy person on their payroll.

The Coalition government considers the new Work Capability Assessment (WCA) to be a success. It takes this view on the basis that more people are being assessed fit to work. David Cameron, for example, referred to "tens of thousands of claimants of incapacity benefits re-assessed, and found ready for work,"[105] as a laudable thing. That is not the measure of success. The measure of success is the number of people who are assessed correctly, the first time round. The old Incapacity Benefit (now replaced by Employment and Support Allowance) assessed 37% of

---

[104] Waddell, 2006, Is work good for your health and well-being? DWP
[105] PM David Cameron, 25th June 2012, Welfare speech

claimants as fit to work. The new WCA assesses 55% of people as fit to work.[106] How have so many people spontaneously become well? There was a reason these people were assessed as unwell under the old system. It was because they really were unwell.

These people have not suddenly become well. Instead, the assessment criteria have become harsher. The Personal Capability Assessment (PCA) used for Incapacity Benefit was already one of the toughest in the world, as recognised by the OECD.[107] Yet the government has decided to make it even tougher by rolling out the WCA nationwide. The PCA awarded 15 points if a person could not walk 50m without needing to stop at least once; for the WCA it must be at least twice ('repeatedly'). The PCA had a whole set of descriptors awarding different amounts of points according to one's ability to go up and down steps; the WCA awards no points if a person can manage two or more steps, even if using a handrail is necessary for those two steps (and many places won't have a handrail). A person who 'cannot walk more than 400m on level ground without stopping or severe discomfort' was awarded 3 points under PCA; under WCA, a person able to walk over 200m (regardless of how difficult this is) receives no points.

To know whether or not the current WCA is working, we need to know both the false positive (i.e., what proportion of claimants are assessed as needing benefits when in fact they do not) and the false negative (who is incorrectly turned down). No one has studied this, so no information is available. However some data can give a good insight into the situation.

When a system works well, appeals against decisions should only occur in marginal cases. In the case of the

---

[106] ESA: Outcomes of WCAs, Great Britain – new claims July 2012., DWP 55% of claims that are not closed before a decision is made. In 2009, 65% of new ESA claimants were found fit for work. There has been a steady decline since then, which is to be hoped is due to improvements in the ESA assessment decision making process.

[107] Organisation for Economic Co-operation and Development, 2003, Transforming disability into ability, policies to promote work and income security for disabled people

WCA, the only people appealing should be those who received just under the required points. After all, most people know whether or not they can walk 200m, dress themselves, prepare a meal, remember to take all their medicine etc. They won't appeal if they can appreciate that the decision was fair (n.b. fraud in DLA costs a mere 0.5% of DLA payments, less than the cost of official error. Fraud in Incapacity Benefit is even lower at 0.3%. ESA will not be assessed until 2013).[108] Yet up to February 2010, 60% of appeals overturned in favour of the claimant were for cases that had originally been awarded *zero* points. A further 23% had been awarded between 3 and 6 points (there are no 1 or 2 point descriptors), leaving just 17% who had been awarded between 7 and 14 points.[109] This is unacceptable; a high percentage of claimants are failing to come close to having a proper assessment of their health made.

Out of all applicants for ESA, 55% are turned down. Of those turned down, 41% go on to appeal.[110] It is not known how many of the remaining 59% reapply, are made too ill, stressed or disillusioned by the process to continue, or were correctly assessed as not needing support. However, for those initially found fit for work at most only 28% are in work (through a previous employer, new employer or self-employment) twelve to eighteen months later. Those who appeal and are again found fit for work may well be expected to be even less likely to be in employment six months later. This does not suggest that the initial 55% found fit for work is an accurate assessment of their true ability to work.

Of those who do appeal, 34% win.[111] If the claimant is represented by another person than the overturn rate is 70%.[112] These are not figures that indicate a high right-

---

108 DWP, 2012, Fraud and Error in the Benefit System

109 HC Deb, 28 June 2011, c662W

110 ESA: Outcomes of WCAs, Great Britain – new claims July 2012., DWP

111 ibid. This is the latest figure for appeals, where the claim started in Dec 2010-Feb 2011. The next quarter has a lower success rate (31%) but only 28% of appeals had been heard.

112 Dryburgh, Unfit for Purpose, 2010, Citizen's Advice Scotland

first-time rate. In some areas it is higher – Oxfordshire Welfare Rights claims to have overturned 93% of ESA decisions at appeal,[113] and a CAB volunteer interviewed by Panorama cited a 100% success rate. This suggests that some people may be turned down not because they are healthy but because they lack appropriate advice.

A recent Citizen's Advice Bureau report concluded that, "The need for an evaluation of the accuracy of WCA reports is continually reinforced in evidence from Citizens Advice Bureaux: A client of a bureau in the North East won her appeal tribunal after a very short hearing. The judge of the tribunal produced – without request – a statement of reasons for his decision, which included the following comment: "The report is misleading, superficial and shallow. It is not fit for purpose... It is inexcusable that the Secretary of State should seek to justify this report as a basis for making a decision. Sadly there are too many reports of this standard." ... In view of the many concerns that have been raised over the years, about the quality of the assessments and the detrimental effects to claimants' health and well-being if they are wrongly assessed, we believe that there should be independent quality assurance of contractors carrying out assessments on behalf of the DWP."[114]

The WCA has been criticised by many professionals, as well as the judge mentioned above. The British Medical Association voted for an end to the WCA with immediate effect. Another judge, asked to consider issues with the WCA in relation to mental health problems, described the assessment as "pretty crude" across the board.[115]

The WCA has also been condemned for its inability to deal with mental health issues or conditions that fluctuate, such as MS, ME and Parkinson's Disease. "After considering the issues in more detail in his second annual

---

[113] Evans, 30th April 2012, Judged fit for work after case reviews, The Oxford Mail.
[114] Pearlman, Royston and Silk, 2012, Right First Time, Citizen's Advice Bureau
[115] Gentleman, Judge considers judicial review of Work Capability Assessment, 29th June 2012, The Guardian

independent review, Professor Harrington concluded that the WCA descriptors needed to be more multi-dimensional, in particular taking into account frequency, severity and duration of symptoms. He also recommended that the criteria were clearly worded to encompass claimants' ability to complete activities 'reliably, repeatedly and safely' and, where appropriate, 'within a reasonable amount of time.' It is clear from Professor Harrington's second report that there remains considerable difficulty in agreeing descriptors and the assessment process in relation to fluctuating conditions (and also for mental, cognitive and learning disability descriptors) in relation to the WCA." [116,117] On 26th July 2012, a judge gave permission for a judicial hearing to be carried out against the Secretary of State for Work and Pensions, on the grounds that it does not reasonably adjust for the difficulties faced by those with mental health conditions.

Recently, the DWP was criticised by the National Audit Office based on its contract with Atos. The DWP was criticised for not penalising Atos for delays in carrying out WCA. Tom Greatrex, a Labour MP, wrote to the NAO to ask for an investigation into the contract between the DWP and Atos. He said, "This is a damning assessment of the failure of the Tory-Liberal government to get value for money for the taxpayer or properly hold Atos to account for the chaos and confusion at the heart of the work capability assessment. The taxpayer is effectively paying for this service twice – yet the government has failed to claw this money back from Atos."[118]

So what can we conclude?

Quite simply, the assessment process is not fit for purpose. Already one of the harshest in the developed world, the previous Labour government made it harsher

---

[116] Professor Malcolm Harrington, An Independent Review of the Work Capability Assessment - year two, November 2011, para 24.
[117] Government support towards the additional living costs of working-age disabled people, February 2012. Department of Work and Pensions.
[118] Ramesh, 17th August 2012, NAO criticises Atos benefits contract., The Guardian.

and the Coalition government rolled the assessment out nation-wide before any attempt had been made to check whether or not it was fair and proper. The process relies on the judgement of people who do not have the necessary medical expertise, or knowledge of the claimant and his or her health. It requires a judgement to be made in far too short a space of time, and the computer program and the method with which it is used are not capable of accurately and reliably assessing a claimant's state of health and ability to work. The questions asked by the assessors bear little relation to the health descriptors and do not provide relevant or logical insight into a claimant's condition. Relevant expert knowledge as provided by the claimant and the health care professionals who have knowledge of the claimant and his or her health, is not given enough weight, if any.

We need people to realise that continuing with the current process is not acceptable. This issue affects not just those who are already unwell, but anyone who may in the future be struck down by a chronic illness, which is everyone.

4

DLA and PIP

Disability Living Allowance was set up to provide for the extra costs that disabled people incur. It is not therefore an out-of-work benefit, and does not act as a disincentive to work. Indeed, many disabled people report that DLA is the means that allows them to work, for example by giving them the financial ability to use a taxi to get to work.

DLA recognises that society presents a large number of barriers to disabled people. The UN defines disability as the barriers in society that make life difficult for disabled people. DLA is therefore a means for society to help remove these barriers. In the long-term it would be better for society to become accessible, but until that society is built disabled people will need individualised support.

DLA is unique in that it is both non-means-tested and does not place any restrictions on how it can be used. Other benefits available for a similar purpose (helping meet the financial costs of being disabled) are means-tested, restricted in usage and/or have to be repaid. DLA therefore remains a vital means of support for people whose disability or chronic illness brings additional costs.

The assessment process for DLA involves filling in a long and detailed questionnaire about your mental and physical health. The DWP decision maker also asks for evidence from the medical professionals involved in the claimant's care and treatment.

The questionnaire starts with 16 pages of notes. It goes on to a further 38 pages and 62 questions. It starts with basic questions about who you are and where you live – including what floor your bedroom and toilet are on. Then there are questions about what illnesses or disabilities you have, what treatment you receive, which health professionals you see, who else is involved in your care, and what aids and adaptations you use. Questions are repeated multiple times – the ability to get around on foot is covered both in the mobility section and in the daily care section; detail on any supervision to guard against danger to self is asked for in both the day and the night care section.

The questions can be divided into different categories. Bodily functions refer to the questions asked in the sections on day and night care. They cover getting in and out of bed, using the toilet, bathing, dressing, eating and drinking, and preparing a cooked meal (if over 16). The next category is supervision to avoid harm to oneself or others. Finally there is the mobility section, which covers the ability to walk and includes needing supervision to remain safe when outdoors on unfamiliar routes.

Filling in the form can be very upsetting. For many people who have spent years trying to mentally minimise their illness or disability, having to bring to mind the true extent to which they are affected can be difficult and emotionally very disturbing. Questions about bodily functions can be distressing, particularly with the knowledge that the form is to be read by a stranger. Detail about supervision to prevent harm can also be very painful; admitting episodes of self-harm and suicidal ideation is not easy, even to close and sympathetic friends.

DLA comes in two components, with differing levels: lower, middle and higher rate care; and lower and higher rate mobility. Mobility refers to the third category mentioned above; care refers to the first two (bodily functions and supervision).

- To get higher rate care, a person must need frequent attention for bodily functions or constant supervision to remain safe during both the day and the night.
- Middle rate care would be applied if either frequent attention or constant supervision were needed, and this was true for the day or the night but not both.
- Lowest rate care is for those who need attention for bodily functions for a significant proportion of the day,

but not frequently. It is also given to over-16s who cannot prepare a cooked meal.

- Lower rate mobility is given to people who can walk, but need guidance or supervision most of the time when in unfamiliar places outdoors.
- Higher rate mobility is for those who are unable or virtually unable to walk. Distance, speed, time and manner of walking are all considered.

Those who are deaf, blind and need someone with them when outdoors also qualify for this higher rate, as do people who have had amputations or been born with no legs from at least the ankle down. It also goes to those who have severe mental impairments, severe behavioural problems and also get highest rate care. Finally, higher rate mobility is given to those for whom walking would cause a deterioration in health.

DLA was designed to replace Attendance Allowance for anyone who became disabled or chronically ill whilst under-65. The London Borough of Lambeth, in its written evidence to the Work and Pensions Committee, pointed out that, "Snapshot opinions from a medical viewpoint, not informed by full knowledge of the disability or even medical history, often lie at the heart of poor decision making. The decision to replace AA with DLA was taken because of acknowledgement of the failure of such medical assessments."[119] The decision to replace DLA with a system that uses such a process, recognised as flawed for AA and highly controversial for ESA, does not appear to be a decision that fits with an aim of ensuring accuracy.

DLA has a 40% initial success rate. Like ESA, it is bugged by inaccuracy; however in this case the face-to-face assessment cannot be blamed. Appeal success for DLA runs at 45%, even higher than that for ESA; with a representative such as a CAB volunteer appeal success reaches 67%. Disability organisations therefore agree that DLA needs reform, but for a different reason to the

---

[119] Written evidence submitted by London Borough of Lambeth to the Work and Pensions Committee. According to Social Welfare Training, it is the most under claimed of all the benefits.

government. The government wants reform because the bill is too high; organisations want reform because the current process is inaccurate.

DLA payments cost £12.6 billion when it was last measured in 2004/05. Of this, 0.5% was due to fraud, 0.6% was due to customer error, and the biggest overpayment was due to official error, at 0.8%. Whilst there are some overpayments due to customer error, errors by customers are much more likely to result in underpayments; £300 million (2.4%) is underpaid due to customer error. Official error also causes some underpayment, but this is only 0.1%. This means that if the government is concerned with accuracy it would do better to tackle customer and official error than fraud. Overall this would result in a slight increase in payments, as the amount not paid due to error exceeds the amount overpaid due to fraud and error combined.

Reform of DLA

The government gives five reasons why reform of DLA is necessary:

1 The number of claimants has increased by 38% since 2002, and the overall caseload is too high.

2 DLA is a disincentive to work. Too many recipients believe it is an out-of-work benefit or believe they will receive less money if they return to work.

3 There should not be automatic entitlement to DLA for some conditions.

4 Where aids are used, these should be taken into account.

5 Changes in circumstances result in over and under payments.[120]

Whilst the number of claimants has risen, it is important to look at why this increase has occurred. The government is changing DLA only for working-age adults;

[120] Disability Living Allowance reform, 2010, Department of Work and Pensions.

when pensioners are excluded, the rise in DLA claims is just half as much, at 19%. Most of this comes from addressing mental health and learning difficulties, which are being increasingly diagnosed in this and all other western countries. There are therefore good reasons why DLA expenditure is increasing.

DLA is not a disincentive to work. It is, as said earlier, not an out-of-work benefit; currently it is not means-tested. This means that anyone whose life is recognised by the government as made more costly through their disability or chronic illness receives DLA. If the government is concerned that people incorrectly believe DLA is an out-of-work benefit, they could quite simply make the truth more widely publicised. To cite DLA as a disincentive to work is wrong.

The government wants to remove automatic entitlement. At the moment, automatic entitlement goes to people with the following conditions: severe visual impairment; 80% deaf and 100% blind; severe mental impairment; double amputees; renal dialysis carried out at home; and less than 6 months to live. In theory, this is so that each case can be looked at individually and therefore be based on "the impact of the impairment or health condition, rather than basing the decision on the health condition or impairment itself." However, the assessment process that has been proposed appears to be heavily focussed on the health condition or impairment, and not on the societal barriers that remain. The government is therefore at risk of carrying out many costly and unnecessary assessments.

Aids may help; but they remain unreliable and expensive. "Many must buy adaptations or improvements to their mobility aids. Others cite maintenance and insurance as further costs. Furthermore the aids don't work all of the time or in all circumstances. Hills, bad weather, pain, or simply broken equipment all present problems. Thus even with aids such as a wheelchair, mobility is still greatly restricted and mobility costs still much greater than non-disabled people. It is a source of great concern that people who can use a manual wheelchair on a flat surface may be deemed completely 'mobile.'"[121]

Whilst changes in circumstances do affect the amount of benefit that is correctly paid, this remains a small proportion. It also remains the case that the majority of incorrect payments are under-payments, at £300 million. Maria Miller, the minister for disability, cites overpayments as £600 million per year. Legally, this is not true; she is referring to changes in circumstances that are so gradual that the point at which entitlement changed cannot be identified. More frequent reassessments would help to clarify this, although it would have to be considered whether the number of appeals, the cost of more frequent assessments, and the stress to applicants is worth the money that would be saved.

The new benefit, replacing DLA only for working-age claimants, is called Personalised Independence Payments (PIP). The government's objectives for the reform are to:

- create a benefit that supports disabled people to overcome the barriers that prevent their leading a full and independent life
- ensure expenditure is sustainable and focussed on those with the greatest barriers, and
- be more accurate, objective and transparent in assessing who would benefit most from support.[122]

Focussing on sustainable expenditure sounds laudable, but when combined with the amount that is under-claimed[123] and the government's plan to cut 20% from the DLA budget, it sounds rather more like limiting support *a priori*. True support should be focussed on what is needed

[121] Campbell, Marsh, Franklin, Gaffney, Dixon, James, Barnett-Cormack, Fon-James, Willis, et al 2012 Responsible Reform; response to Question 8 'Should the assessment of a disabled person's ability take into account any aids and adaptations they use?

[122] Disability Living Allowance Reform – Impact Assessment, 2011, DWP; Paragraph 10.

[123] Written evidence submitted by the London Borough of Lambeth to the DWP. "It has been suggested that, despite this work, take up is as low as 50%."

and who needs it. If the government thinks it cannot afford to support disabled people it should say so, rather than claim to support people whilst simultaneously reducing support. It is worth remembering that social security on a nation-wide level and the creation of the NHS both occurred immediately post-WW2, a time of poverty.

The government cannot focus PIP on those with the greatest barriers if it defines barriers as physical, mental or cognitive, rather than as barriers in society. The greatest barriers often arise from "social, practical and environmental factors like inaccessible public transport, unsuitable housing and lack of access to informal support from family, friends, neighbours, etc."[124] If the government continues to ignore these barriers then it will not achieve its objective of helping disabled people overcome these barriers, and nor it will target those who face the biggest barriers. It will also fail to be accurate.

Relying on an 'objective' test that uses only a points-based, tick box approach will not capture the full details of a person's needs.[125] It is likely to run into the same problems faced by the Work Capability Assessment for Employment and Support Allowance, in which people can be told 'I cannot make you fit the system,' and which has a high incorrect rejection rate. These problems as identified with the WCA are likely to be found with PIP when it is brought in. "The assessment for PIP needs to be empathetic and avoid the mechanistic, box-ticking approach initially used in the WCA... The Committee is concerned that the current draft criteria on which the assessment will be based are still too reliant on a 'medical model' of disability. Such a model may fail to take sufficient account of the impact of social, practical and environmental factors, such as housing and access to public transport, on disabled people's ability to participate in society and the additional costs they therefore incur."[126] Illnesses and disabilities are highly complex. Any one

[124] The Future of PIP: a social model based approach, 2011, Scope
[125] ibid.
[126] Government support towards the additional living costs of working-age disabled people. Work and Pensions Committee, 7th Report, 2012

condition can vary from person to person; any one person can have very different combinations of conditions. Trying to fit this into a simplistic, mechanistic test will not be sufficient to achieve an accurate test.

The government has said that it is committed to having a social model of disability to underpin its reform of DLA. By social model, they mean that disability is created by the environment,[127] people's attitudes, and organisational barriers.[128] However, Lord Freud has said that PIP is not a fully social model, nor is it meant to be.[129] Scope, having looked at the criteria in the second draft for PIP, has concluded that this is largely a medical model.[130] The Human Rights Committee corroborated this, saying, "The proposed assessment process for eligibility for PIPs, however, has been criticised for failing to give effect to the Government's stated intention that the assessment process for PIPs takes a more holistic account of the impact of disability, because the test for eligibility provided for in the Bill is essentially a medical one."[131]

The initial draft criteria explicitly stated, "Inability to undertake activities must be due to a physical, mental or cognitive impairment with disabling effects and not simply a matter of preference by the individual."[132] The report by Scope goes into detail on each draft descriptor, discussing its relation to the medical and social models. I will give a summary here.

In relation to the ability to plan and buy food and drink, the descriptors refer to the ability to buy and plan

---

[127] e.g. inaccessible buildings and services

[128] e.g. inflexible policies, practices and procedures

[129] Freud, L quoted in transcript of De Havilland 'Lords Committee Stage – Welfare Reform Bill (Day Thirteen)', De Havilland, 14 Nov 2011

[130] The Future of PIP: a social model based approach, 2011, Scope

[131] Legislative Scrutiny: Welfare Reform Bill, Joint Committee on Human Rights, Twenty-first Report of Session 2010-12; HL Paper 233/HC 1704

[132] Personal Independence Payment: initial draft of assessment criteria - a technical note to support the initial draft of the assessment regulations, May 2011, DWP

unaided; buy only with continual prompting; plan only with continual prompting; and plan only with continual assistance. This is heavily medical. Barriers arising from society are not considered, but include: buying specialist food stuffs, which often are expensive; paying for private transport to shops or paying delivery charges and being restricted to minimum spends; inability to compare with cheaper shops; and paying for food and drink for a carer, which may not be covered in a social care plan.

Preparing a meal does not take into account family responsibilities (a disabled lone parent may not be able to prepare meals for the entire family) or the accessibility of the kitchen and height of the oven and work surfaces – being able to bend down to an oven is not necessary, according to PIP. This also means that no money will be provided to convert a kitchen into one that is accessible.

The descriptors for taking medicine and treatment do not consider the treatment and medications not available on the NHS, or that people on PIP may not qualify for means-tested free prescriptions. Many 'prescription' therapies are available on prescription for short-term use only. Cost for travel to therapies also has to be borne by the claimant.

Ability to communicate has one of the broadest sets of descriptors suggested for PIP. Still it fails to consider the cost of buying and maintaining communication devices. Indeed the inability to consider the cost of aids and appliances is a major flaw in the government's proposals for PIP.

Difficulties with bathing, grooming and toileting are not always because of an impairment, but rather because of unsuitable housing. Utility bills may be higher because of a need to engage in bathing or washing clothes more frequently. Bathing and grooming does not, under PIP, extend to the legs and feet. There is therefore no contribution towards the costs of paying for feet treatment, such as washing feet and cutting toenails. The ability to dress does not consider the cost of having to buy specialist clothing or buy new clothes more frequently.

"Limiting movement to ability to cover 200 metres – half an athletics track – with or without the use of a manual aid, suggests a very limited vision of the issues disabled people face when getting out and about." The descriptors for mobility fail to consider the accessibility of public transport. They also do not consider the cost of purchasing and maintaining aids and appliances for assisting with mobility.

The government's proposals therefore are hugely flawed by non-incorporation of societal barriers. Adapting one's home, purchasing and maintaining aids, transport, access to treatment, utilities bills, adequate nutrition, adequate personal hygiene – these are not covered in the government's proposals

The government has repeatedly said that there will be support for the 'most needy.' Disability organisations, however, agree that need is not an accurate measure of cost. Claudia Wood, of Demos, said that, "If we reserve it just for people with the greatest needs, there are going to be people there who have complex conditions who may have very well adapted homes, a partner who supports them and accessible transport, and do not necessarily have huge living costs. So there is a mismatch on the targeting there, and that could be inefficient for the Government. It is not just about people with low needs and high costs, but also about people with high needs and low costs getting more than they necessarily need."

There is consensus amongst these organisations that these strong recommendations - for incorporating better means of assessing disability-related costs - have not been incorporated. In response to this, the Government argued that many such costs "have already been taken into account within the proxy of impact of impairments," and that, "individuals who have difficulties getting out are likely to have higher utility bills, while those who need support planning a journey and moving about are likely to have higher transport costs."[133] Scope responds, "We are unsatisfied with this explanation. An individual who is

[133] Personal Independence Payment: second draft of assessment criteria, 2012, DWP

incontinent – even intermittently so – is likely to have very high utility bills from increased washing and drying but may experience relatively few problems getting out and about. Alternatively, an individual may be able to prepare food and drink, but, because of their condition, require a particular diet, which may well result in extra costs. We believe it is very risky to assume that problems a disabled person experiences in one area will be readily brought to light by an assessment or descriptor that focuses on another. Worryingly, such an approach risks homogenising the plethora of barriers that disabled people face in their daily lives."[134]

A report by the Human Rights Committee said that, "The duty of progressive realisation in UN human rights treaties entails a strong presumption against retrogressive measures affecting the right to social security and to an adequate standard of living. The committee is therefore not satisfied that the Government has demonstrated reasonable justification for the negative impact of the introduction of Personal Independence Payments on the right of disabled people to independent living." The report also concluded that "amending the Bill to ensure that the assessment process for PIPs takes account of the social, practical and environmental barriers experienced by disabled claimants would make it less likely that the Bill will lead to incompatibilities with the UK's obligations under the UNCRDP."[135]

The Human Rights Committee further said that, "The Government's view is that the proposal to replace DLA with PIPs is compliant with the UK's obligations under the UNCRDP. It says that PIP is intended to target resources on the people that need it most, taking into account the whole range of services available to, and balancing the various needs of, disabled people. It believes that the changes are justifiable, in terms of supporting those most

---

[134] The Future of PIP: a social model based approach, 2011, Scope

[135] Legislative Scrutiny: Welfare Reform Bill, 2011, Joint Committee on Human Rights, Twenty-first Report of Session 2010-12; HL Paper 233/HC 1704

affected by disability and introducing a fairer, more consistent and evidence-based, assessment system to identify such individuals. However, the proposed 20% reduction in the overall budget for PIP means that funds are not merely being refocused on the most needy, but are being significantly reduced."

The government needs to be very careful with its proposals for PIP. It is relying heavily on a medical model when experts agree that a social model is needed, and it is pushing ahead with plans for a face-to-face assessment. This is despite the flaws in this process that led to DLA being created to replace Attendance Allowance, and the problems that are still occurring with the similarly-assessed Employment and Support Allowance.

Furthermore, the government may be at risk of breaching human rights.

Conclusion

The majority of people in the UK want the government to support people who are sick and disabled. But many may have been misled by government and media misrepresentation. Frequent references to people being abandoned or festering on benefits, or the many people whom we all know are claiming sickness-related benefits when they could work, perpetuates the myth that the benefit system is rife with fraud and undeserving recipients.

The reality is the opposite. As I have shown, fraud is tiny. At the same time, tens of thousands of people are being denied the money they merit and so desperately need. Even where benefits are given, it is often insufficient to meet their needs.

The government has plans to change the system, but not for the better. The process for assessing ESA claimants is being kept, despite the evidence that it doesn't work. DLA is being scrapped – but only for working age people. The assessment process for these people is being changed to one that is harsher and is carried out in a similar manner to ESA. This means DLA assessments for working-age people are returning to a format that was known not to work when DLA was Attendance Allowance, and which continues not to work with ESA.

Part 2

Life in the Slow Lane

Preface to Life in the Slow Lane

Society continues to be disabling.

As the stories in Part 2 will show, there are many ways in which society places a burden on those with long-term impairments or illnesses.

The disabilities caused by society have not greatly lessened over the years. Some may never be able to be mitigated; others, such as access for wheelchair users, have more obvious solutions.

But in the meantime it is vital that those who struggle for medical reasons to participate fully in society, either as a provider or a consumer, are given the support they need from the rest of society.

5

Brian's Story: At the Throw of a Dice

I used to be a lorry driver. I worked for a year doing night shifts, delivering fruit and veg. It was hard work – the crates would be loaded using a fork lift but largely had to be removed manually. The hours weren't great either. I would start work at 2am and still be at it after 11am. When I got back home I would want to go straight to bed, so my wife would take our young son out for a couple of hours to let me have some quiet. It made me feel disconnected from my family.

Because of the lack of time with my family, I changed jobs. My new job was delivering linen to hotels. This was a 6am start, and would finish any time between 12noon and 6pm. It was the service that was important, rather than the hours worked. This meant that on days when I completed all my rounds early, I could take extra deliveries on overtime. It was very important to me that I provide for my family and avoid needing any government support.

The work still meant I missed out on my young family. Every other weekend I worked Saturdays, and on Sundays I was involved with church activities. I would have liked to have more time to spend with my wife and by then two children, but this wasn't possible if I were to provide for my family financially. I considered it important to clear the debt that had come with my marriage, and I was delighted when my hours of work finally got me into the clear. I was the epitome of Cameron's 'We're all in it together,' – losing many hours with my family in order to be able to pay for them and not need to seek government support. I was proud of what I had achieved and of my ability to provide for my family.

But then the illness came. Out of nowhere, from no reason or logic. It could have been anyone; it was me. There was nothing I could have done about it. There is nothing you can do to prevent the same thing happening to you. It is no fault of mine that I became ill; no merit of yours that you have not.

At first I felt a little odd, just a bit off-colour at the beginning of the week that my illness struck, but as the week went on I was losing strength quite quickly. I was concerned by this, but thought a rest over the weekend would be enough for me to get back to normal. This didn't happen. I felt so bad that after the weekend I took a day off work to go see a doctor. He gave me some tablets to take which helped a bit, so I went back to work on Wednesday. I wasn't quite right but I was ex-army, and we got on with the job regardless.

Wednesday was always the busiest day. There were a lot of heavy deliveries to make, and I was beginning to realise that this might not be something I could get over by willpower and determination. With my body not fully recovered I found each delivery more and more tiring. By the last delivery my left leg felt very tight, as though I had pulled a muscle in the calf, and I was limping. It was a massive relief to finish my deliveries and drive back to the depot, 40 minutes away. When I arrived my leg was much worse and my boss was concerned, but I thought it was just a pulled muscle so told him I was okay and didn't need more time off. I was still refusing to accept that this might be something more serious, even though at the back of my mind that awareness was present.

Back at home, I started dragging my leg and tripping over my foot. I decided to have a restful evening rather than go to our church small-group meeting, and expected that this would be enough for me to get through work the next day. Instead, I woke up with the whole of my left leg a deadweight, as though a lump of lead were tied to it. Stubborn as ever, I made my way downstairs (sat on my bottom) and got my work bag packed. I managed to hobble out to my car, got in and turned the key in the ignition. I put the clutch down to get the car into first – and nothing happened. I couldn't push down the clutch. I tried again, and still no movement. It was thoroughly bizarre and a little frightening.

I tried a few times but there was no movement. Giving in was not something I do, but even I could tell that I could not drive today, and as my work involved driving I also could not work. Having finally worked this out, I called my boss and told him what had happened, or rather what had not happened. With the day off work and now quite worried that such bizarre symptoms were occurring, I took a bus to see my doctor. The stop was only 5 minutes' walk away, but with my leg dragging it took three times as long.

My doctor was very surprised to see me again so soon. He tried getting a response from the nerves below my knee by tapping with his hammer, but nothing happened. The doctor looked very concerned; he was tutting and shaking his head in a way that did not suggest a simple answer to my problem. He said I would need to go to hospital for a full check-up and rang ahead for me to let the hospital know I was coming. He also gave me a medical card to take with me to A & E. I told my wife it was just a precaution, that there was nothing seriously wrong – still as ever refusing to 'give in,' be a 'slacker.'

At the hospital I explained what was happening to me and a nurse took my blood. After some time in the waiting room, a doctor came for me and I had to say yet again what was going on. He repeated the tests my GP had done earlier that morning, then told me to go back to the waiting room. My wife was with me and she looked exhausted and strained, having to deal with a baby and the uncertainty of what was going on with her husband.

Before too long another nurse came. I thought I would have to repeat my story, but instead was told that I was to be admitted to the medical assessment ward. I was terrified, and my wife's face showed the same fear. I thought I knew how to handle fear from my time in the armed forces, but this was very different. During active service I had known what was happening and what dangers existed. Now I knew nothing.

I felt guilty and sad. My little boy would come home from school and I would not be there. It would be terrifying for him, to find that the dad he had looked up to and depended upon was suddenly unable to be with him.

It was difficult saying goodbye to my wife and baby, knowing how much my wife was suffering and being unable to help in any way. I felt guilty for being ill and causing trouble; sad for being unable to do anything about it or bring any relief to my wife and children.

That first night was terrifying. I had no idea what was wrong with me or what would happen. My strength was rapidly fading – would it go completely? Would it ever return? Would I be able to eat, to breathe, if I lost any more strength?

My legs were being taken over. It was a strange sensation, hot with pins and needles. To get to the toilet that evening I needed support from a nurse. The next day I couldn't get up, I had no strength at all. It meant I couldn't use the toilet at all, so a nurse brought me a bottle and funnel to use. It was embarrassing, even with the curtains around my bed. The nurses' station was only a few feet away. But there was nothing I could do about that.

Throughout the day more and more of my body shut down, as though fuses were blowing all over my body. There was no reset option. It was frightening to be so totally out of control; unable to control this mysterious illness and unable to control my body. Bit by bit I was losing strength and losing the ability to move.

The next night – Thursday – my back muscles were twitching and spasming as though they were having a party all to themselves. When I woke up I could move only my head and eyes. Everything else had stopped. I had to be spoon fed, washed, shaved and dressed by the nurses. I was completely unable to do anything for myself. I tried so hard, willing my fingers to move, but willpower was useless here. When my wife came I cried, and could not wipe my tears away.

I still had not been told what was wrong with me, indeed the doctors themselves had not confirmed it as I still needed more tests. A medical friend had suggested to me that it might be Guillain-Barre, and that if so it would be good for me to be transferred to another hospital that had good facilities for caring for people with that illness. To our collective pleasure, on Saturday evening I was transferred to that hospital and was taken to the Acute Neurological Unit (ANU). Once I had settled in I was taken off for a CT scan and a lumbar puncture. The scan was unbelievably noisy and uncomfortable. Then I had the lumbar puncture, and realised the scan was not uncomfortable at all! I could feel the needle for the puncture pressing into my spine. It was not pleasant.

My sleep that night was very disturbed. I was in quite a bit of pain and for a long time that kept me awake. And the mattress was odd. It was an air mattress, designed to prevent pressure sores, and it was constantly humming and moving around beneath me. Opposite me one of my ward mates was constantly getting out of bed or moving around; he seemed to be much more used to being awake at night rather than during the day, and this did not help me sleep.

Early in the morning I woke in severe pain. My call bell had been placed where I could butt it with my head, but it had shifted since then. I had to call out for a nurse, although I was worried about waking the other people in the room, but my pain was too great. The nurse came soon, but there was nothing she could give me except Paracetamol, as no doctors had prescribed me any medicine yet. She brought me a flow meter as well, asking me to blow into it as hard and as fast as I could, to measure how well my lungs were working. I scored 4.8 litres, which was okay but lower than the 6+ litres typical for a man of my age.

The pain relief didn't do very much and I found it difficult to get back to sleep. Eventually I did get some sleep, only to be woken by a doctor at 5am. She had the test results back, telling me that I did have Guillain-Barre syndrome. This is caused by an immune response, sometimes to a bacteria or virus but more often without any known cause. The immune system becomes over-active and continues after the initial trigger has gone, attacking the peripheral nervous system and thus causing a loss of ability to send messages along the nerves.

Guillain-Barre is treated by reducing the body's attack on the nerves. This is done either by filtering antibodies out of the blood, or by injecting immunoglobulins (Igs) into the veins. I had three bottles of Igs administered to me each day, and with each costing £300 I felt I was suddenly a very important person! Igs are proteins involved in the immune system. Doctors do not fully understand how this works; it may be that injecting Igs helps to clear the abnormal antibodies that are causing the symptoms. Physiotherapy is also used to help restore muscle function. Most people make a full recovery within a year, but 10-20% are left with permanent problems such as weakness and pain, or even blindness. 5% die as a result of breathing problems, other infections or problems with the heart.

I was set up with an intra-venous drip to have the Igs injected into me. The machine attached to the drip clicked every few seconds with a sound like a possessed chicken. This added to the groans and hisses of the air mattress and the beeps of other machines in the room, making a mini and very annoying percussion group!

Guillain-Barre is a rare illness, affecting 1-2 in 100 000. This made me quite an interest to the medical students, adding to my importance. They would crowd around my bed, led by their supervisor, and be asked to identify my illness. It was certainly interesting watching them trying to work it out! With all my pain and paralysis, it was a small comfort to think that I was useful to someone.

The pain I was in was increasing and I wasn't coping very well. I was constantly calling the nurses to ask if they could do something. Most often they would tell me I had to wait a couple of hours before taking any more painkillers. It was very frustrating. The nurses were always very understanding and would move me to a different position to try to relieve the pain, but nothing really helped. The nurses spent a lot of time with me, either changing my position or checking my breathing with the flow metre. They had to change TV channels for me as well. My family paid for the cards, which cost about £2.50 a day. It was good to have something to take my mind off myself but I have never watched much TV and was rarely interested in anything that was on.

By Wednesday morning, 8 days after my admission, my score on the peak flow had fallen to 2 litres. It wasn't good, and each time I had to do it I was completely exhausted afterwards. It continued to fall during the day. It was a dangerous situation to be in, and took a lot of my strength out of me just to do the test. When my mum came in to see me, I was so tired I lay with my eyes closed most of the time. I was desperate to not waste the time when people could visit, but I simply did not have the strength to talk much.

That evening my peak flow had fallen to 1.3 litres. The nurse told me I would have to be transferred to intensive care (IC), as I would need to be ventilated if my breathing worsened. My wife was with me at the time and I could she how worried she was. She held my hand whilst we waited for some hospital staff to come to transfer me to IC. I was terrified too; I had thought the illness would stabilise soon and then improve. To be told I had to be on IC was very scary. I had no idea now how bad I would get. I knew I could die, and was desperate for my wife and young children that I would recover.

On IC, a doctor came to see me. To his concern – and mine when I knew - my face had dropped on one side. It was possible that this had been caused by a mini stroke, but the doctor was able to confirm that it was just part of my illness. This was not much better news, as I should not have continued to deteriorate when I had been on Igs for almost four days. He did prescribe a new drug to try to control my pain, which I was grateful for, but he advised me that it might take several days to have an effect.

A nurse came to hook me up to various machines. One was oxygen. It was incredible being on it. I hadn't realised how bad my breathing had become, but now I felt so much better. A physiotherapist then brought another machine (the 'bird') to help my breathing. I had to breathe in as far as I could and then let the machine do the rest. The machine did most of the work but even so I was exhausted after a few breaths. The physio then massaged my chest which was hugely painful but necessary to keep my chest clear.

I was left to get some rest, but rest was not going to come that night! All the machines around me made a lot of noise and I was still in a lot of pain, not helped by the physio's efforts! Part way through the night a pad came off and the machine attached to it panicked, sending out high pitched alarm noises. The nurses rushed over, alert to a crisis, but calm returned as soon as I explained what had happened. My breathing now was stable at 1.3l, but a doctor who came to see me said that if it did deteriorate further I would be put into an induced coma and go on full life support. It was a nervous time.

The physios continued to use the bird every day, hoping that this would prevent my needing ventilation. I had been given leg splints as well to prevent my muscles from shortening. I tried to persuade the physios that I did not need them, but wasn't listened to! So I had to cope with the cramps and pains that they brought on. I had problems with my hands too. My fingers had curled up almost to a fist and I couldn't straighten them. The therapists worked on them for half an hour before managing to get them fully open, then gave me splints for my hands as well, adding to my pain.

That night I had to wear a patch over my left eye as I could no longer close it. With all my machines and contraptions it was very difficult to sleep. The nurses came every few hours to check my breathing and several times I did not manage to sleep between two checks. But my breathing was slowly improving, which was excellent news and pleased my consultant greatly. Most people who get as bad as I did end up on artificial ventilation.

My breathing stabilised on the intensive care unit (ICU) and then started to improve. Two days later when my doctor came to check up on me he was very pleased that I had recovered so much and said that I could move back to the ANU ward. The physios had added more routines for me to go through with their help, and were now trying to get me sat up for a couple of minutes. It required four of them and drained away what little energy I had very quickly. During my third week in hospital the physios decided to try getting me sitting in a wheelchair. They had to use a hoist to transfer me from the hospital bed to the wheelchair. At first I had a time limit of 30 minutes in the chair, as any longer would be too exhausting for me. Getting back into the bed at the end of that time was bliss. That simple act of sitting – something most of us do to rest – was a massive drain on me. It was such a weird sensation to be in so much pain from sitting. I had all the restrictions of a quadriplegic being trapped in my own body, but unlike them I could feel pain.

By the end of the fourth week my face was recovering a little so I no longer needed an eye patch. I was also well enough to be moved onto the rehabilitation ward. I was sad to be leaving my bed-neighbour whom I had shared many jokes with. His wife had come in often to see him and would bring him chocolates. She would share these with me, and we would make jokes about her hand-feeding another man.

I hoped that in the new ward I would get more rest. On ANU, I had mentally christened the man in the bed opposite to mine 'Jack', because like a Jack-in-the-box he was constantly popping out of bed only to be put firmly back by nurses. He had kept me awake as much as the pain had. Sadly my hope was not realised. A man on my new ward with me was often awake in the night and would call loudly for a nurse several times. It made getting rest even more difficult, but I was sorry for him, as he seemed confused and not aware that he was in hospital.

To my pleasure, a few days after my transferral my friend from the ANU ward was moved to the bed next to mine on the rehabilitation ward. Having him there was wonderful for keeping me from getting depressed as we joked and laughed a lot. His wife continued to look after me too, always getting me a drink or something to eat when she came to visit.

Some weeks later I was trying to move my fingers, something I did every day with no effect, and was amazed to see them move a little. I called my friend over to check and he agreed, they were moving. When a nurse came in I called her over as well to show off. Every visitor I had that day was made to watch as well. I was so excited, like a young boy who has just learned a new trick and now wants to show off to everyone he can. It was incredible to be able to move again. I felt I was starting to recover and would eventually be no longer trapped inside something that is human shape but feels totally alien.

I continued to make slow progress. Movement was coming back to my arms, so I could now just about turn the pages in a book or magazine. My movement wasn't very good and I often ripped the pages out accidentally. I needed glasses to read, but couldn't lift my arms to put them on my face. I sorted this by opening the arms of the glasses, and putting them in their case on my table. By leaning forward I could get my head down and slide the glasses on. It was quite a challenge!

I now had to work on rehabilitating my whole body. A physio came to score me, on a scale of 1-5 where 5 is very good. I scored 1 or 2 all over. My new physio was excited to get to work with someone who needed full-body rehabilitation, rather than just one part. I suppose I should have been glad to provide interest for him, but really I just wanted to get some mobility back. My left arm was working better than my right, so I was trying to learn to write left-handed. This would be a challenge in normal circumstances, but with my loss of strength it was even harder. I could just about hold a pen with my left hand but not at all with my right. My left arm has continued to improve faster than my right, so I have remained left-handed.

As I improved I became able, with the help of some foam aids, to feed myself. Some things were still impossible. Mashed potato, for instance, was of too thick a consistency for me to be able to push a fork into it. But I was amazed at the incredible intricacy of the human body and what it is capable of. Such little acts astounded me and I delighted in each movement I could make. Even when I had to give up in exhaustion, as often happened after several attempts to turn a page, still I found what the healthy body can do was wonderful.

One day my physio decided it was time for me to work on standing up. In the gym I sat on the end of a plinth with assistants around me. I tried on my own at first. Counting down I prepared myself like an athlete getting ready for a sprint, and on 'go' I summoned up everything I had to stand up. I remained seated, yet felt I had never exerted so much energy before in my life. After a rest, I tried again, this time with two assistants beside me to push up from my waist and one in front to straighten my knees. For a few moments I was stood and felt like a giant, I hadn't viewed anything from such a high position in several months. I was elated (and exhausted) for the rest of the day.

My recovery continued but my hands were still far behind my arms. I couldn't lift things, and would often knock things on the floor when I was trying to pick them up. This created further problems, as I didn't have the finger strength to press the call button for a nurse to come and get what I needed. Instead I would lift my arm and let it drop with gravity onto the button. It would usually take several attempts before it worked. The health care assistants were always very good about it, and one would joke, 'buzzers are not toys.'

Other movement gradually came back, but at times it was disheartening at how slow my progress was. The physio was also concerned as most people recovered faster and my slow progress increased the chances of permanent damage. Each slight improvement was a milestone to celebrate, but there were so many miles still to go. It was a long time before I was able, when sitting on my bed, to move my back forward from the pillows supporting me. It was weeks after then when, for the first time, I could lie on my bed and lift my legs a little up and down, still keeping my heels resting on the bed. The movement was through my thighs, I had no movement at all below my knees.

A few weeks later the physio tried electrically stimulating my lower legs, but there was no response. I felt a slight tingling, but that was all. To show me what should have happened, the physio stimulated my thigh. That contracted beautifully, and painfully, which is what should happen. The lack of response from my lower leg showed that I had no nerve activity from my knees downwards. There was the possibility that the nerves would regrow, but with each passing week it became less and less likely.

10 months after my admission to hospital I was ready to try walking. The physio brought a walking frame to the gym for me. It had a horseshoe shaped pad for me to lean my arms on, and handles at the front to hold. Most of my weight was carried through the frame. It was a massive effort to stand from my wheelchair to the frame, but I managed it and rested for a few minutes before trying to move. I prepared myself to use all my strength and heaved the frame forward, but before I could move a foot the frame slipped back to its original position. I was disappointed, and also now so tired that I had to sit down again.

I was determined that I would take a step. The physio suggested putting the brakes on, so that the frame wouldn't roll back. So after getting some strength back, I pulled myself up for another attempt. I rested, then tried to again. Still it was not enough. I was so upset, and still set on moving. But I was also scared of falling. I knew this was holding me back, but as these thoughts went through my head I knew I was more afraid of failing than of falling. So with a huge effort and loud grunt I thrust myself forward – and the frame moved! This time it stayed, and with delight I stepped forward into it. I managed another seven 'steps' that day.

I was discharged one week short of a year after being admitted. I had a council house already adapted for a disabled person that I moved straight in to. There was a few weeks wait before any new physios came to see me, and during that time my improvement almost stopped. However once they had come and started me with some exercise I picked up a bit more progress. They also arranged for me to have hydrotherapy once a week, which I loved.

There was still no response below my knees. I had to wear splints to keep my feet positioned correctly, as otherwise they would drop and I would end up dragging my toes across the floor. I needed a zimmer frame to be able to get up and walk at all, and needed to have someone behind me with a wheelchair for when I ran out of strength. The community physios came 1-2 times each week and gradually I picked up strength and dexterity.

That was all several years ago – I came out of hospital in 2009. My consultant thinks it unlikely that I will see any improvement from where I am now. I have no nerve activity below my knees so still need to wear callipers. If I walk without them, I have to lift my legs very high as though I am moon walking to prevent dragging my feet. I can just about get around my house without using crutches, but always use crutches outdoors and prefer to have my wheelchair with me.

Because of my lack of mobility, I have to take aspirin to reduce the likelihood of a blood clot in my legs. I also need to manipulate my ankles each day to prevent them seizing up. The callipers are necessary to prevent my dragging my feet, but these keeps my ankles very rigid, so I have to move them with my hands to keep the joint supple.

My hands are still far from normal. I can't stretch or move my fingers as easily as healthy people can, and an hour of constant use is too much. After that they hurt, a lot, and I lose strength so can't grip. Even when I have not over-worked them, simple things are difficult. Opening screw-top milk bottles always results in the bottle being deformed, as I barely have the strength and grip to combat the lid's determination to stay on. Getting out keys from my pocket is also a problem and it takes several minutes to find the finger position and grip that allows me to pick them up.

I am also still in pain. I have various painkillers but they don't totally remove the pain. I try to go to the gym once a week, but the day after I am always exhausted and in a lot more pain. I want to become strong again, at least strong compared to how I am now, but if I try too hard I make myself worse. I may now be close to the limit of what I can achieve, no matter how hard I work out, but my faith in God keeps me going and I continue to believe that God can heal me. But I know that if I am left with this reminder of my illness, God can still use me to encourage others, so I am not bitter at all.

At the moment I haven't had any trouble receiving government support. I am lucky in that sense. I suppose my disability is so obvious – my callipers, crutches and wheelchair all point to my lack of strength and mobility. I tire very quickly and my whole body, everything I do, has slowed down a lot. Fatigue and pain affects me mentally as well, as my brain stops working properly and my concentration and cognitive abilities go.

I try to write music, as this is something I can be flexible about. I can never guarantee when or how much I can do, which would be far from ideal for an employer! No-one wants to employ a worker who is probably never going to get a piece of work finished on time or to a good enough standard. That is how it would be with me, because fatigue and pain would set in so quickly, rendering me incapable of work.

I never expected any of this. I expected to be a family man, supporting his wife and children through hard work, fully self-dependent. But this illness, like so many things, is random. It is not something I, or you, could have planned for. Right now I need help, both physically and financially. I hope that in the future I will be able to support myself again, but it isn't likely if I don't have any more improvement.

I am determined to do my best, but my best is very limited, and that is not my fault.

6

Aida's Story: Just Plain Lazy

'My New Year's resolution for 2012 was to become disabled. Nothing too serious, maybe just a bit of a bad back or one of those newly invented illnesses which makes you a bit peaky for decades - fibromyalgia, or M.E.' *Rod Liddle, The Sun, 27/1/12*

'I know just what you mean! I haven't had a decent night's rest in over a week! And what with rushing round after the children, and keeping up with all the cooking and cleaning, I'm run off my feet!'

'Tell me about it! I haven't had one evening at home this week. Really I don't know how I do it sometimes!'

'I'm *so* tired. I had to take the children to the dentist, and then my husband 'went sick' when it was his week to do the household chores, and now this! I need a break. Still, that's life. I'll get it done.'

Everyone knows what it's like to be tired. But I know an exhaustion deeper than any tiredness you feel, and a pain beyond your aching feet

I don't wish to complain. I am middle-class and British, which is a good start. I am also female, which can be considered a disadvantage relative to males, but I don't mind that. My parents are still together, have made a good job of bringing me up, and were able – having saved for many years – to pay for me to learn to drive and to contribute to my living expenses whilst I was at university. I am well aware of how lucky I am. I hope that by sharing my story, you can understand that I am not just plain lazy.

I watched my parents anxiously. What would they say? I hoped, so much, it would be the answer I wanted. It was.

That was it. No more school. I was overjoyed. After years of crying at the end of every holiday, years of taunting and mockery, years of burying myself in work to try to hide from myself how much I hated being there – I never had to go back. My twin sister and I could spend the next three years before our GCSEs learning from home.

Now, of course, I had no external pressure to work. No class-mates to compete with, no homework set, no tests to compare myself against. But, I had the desire to learn and the need to maintain good enough standards that my parents would not send me back to school. So I worked and worked. Self-discipline, self-motivation, good timekeeping, good organisation – skills many people do not have even at university. I had them before I was 14. I got myself through eight GCSEs (three of them taken early), one freestanding qualification and one AS-level. I achieved straights As and A-stars. So far was so good, and so far was good enough for an application to Cambridge.

A-levels were now approaching. Science was my passion, but I also loved English Literature and English Language. It narrowed down to a decision between Chemistry and English Literature. Chemistry was more useful, and easier to do – no long quotations, less subjective answers, and a potential for overlap with Physics and Biology. But, English Literature – so interesting, so fascinating; the opportunity to see life through another's eyes, to experience a different reality. I chose Chemistry. To make up for choosing the 'easier' option, I added Further Maths, bringing my A-level haul up to five – two maths, three sciences.

As AS-level exam time drew near, I was spending a lot of my breaks and free hours studying, to avoid having to work at home. I was not nervous, but I have always liked to keep study separated from home – college is for studying, home for relaxing. I've never felt any need to be stressed about exams. They're mostly about 'ticking the boxes' – get in the key words, make one point for each mark and an extra point just to make sure, remember to say 'violet' (which is a particular wavelength on the visible spectrum) and not 'purple' (a mix of blue and red wavelengths). There are a limited number of questions, although they can be phrased in different ways, so if you know the words expected it is possible to get full marks. I was aiming for full marks on the maths papers – they're so quick to do, that anything less would have been tragedy.

When exam results day eventually arrived, after months of trying not to think about matters that I could no longer have any influence on, it was not a disappointment. I had achieved straight As, as expected, and hadn't dropped any UMS marks on any of the maths or biology papers. It was looking good for university applications, which would start as soon as I returned to college for upper sixth. However, I found out during the summer that Cambridge requires a foreign language GCSE – something I hadn't taken – so I had to arrange with my sixth form college to be given lessons once a fortnight for a French GCSE. My personal statement also needed to be written. This didn't pose me any problems; I've never had any difficulty talking about my success (you've probably noticed from reading this!). Once the application was submitted – to read Natural Sciences at Cambridge and at several other universities – it seemed a long wait until the interview in December, and even longer until the reply in January. It was not really long at all; but the anticipation, the longing for an acceptance from Cambridge, stretched the days out to huge lengths, even with Christmas and New Year intervening.

Finally, the envelope arrived – I had been accepted to read Natural Sciences at Peterhouse, Cambridge. It was conditional on four As (although they wouldn't count General Studies, a compulsory A-level at my college) and at least a C in GCSE French. The months seemed to speed by with final exams, results day and confirmation of a place at Cambridge. I was nervous and shy, uncertain of leaving home and my twin sister. I knew it was going to be tough without her.

It was tough. Adjusting to a new place and new people and coping with 30 hours a week of scheduled work is never easy. I thought I would not find it too bad, having managed to get five As (plus an A in General Studies) and French GCSE, so assumed I knew about hard work and long hours! How wrong I was! A-level maths and science specifications detailed everything I needed to know, and the exams had set answers that needed only a bit of familiarity to ensure near-perfection. But at Cambridge there was a description of the topics we needed to know about and there were lecture notes to start us off, but to get the coveted first required more knowledge than was provided by the lecturers. For the first time in my life, I did not know what was expected of me, and I was scared.

Cambridge has a good network of support for its students. They include a Director of Studies, in charge of making sure that you are getting on okay with your work, and a personal tutor, who is there to help with any personal or financial issues. At the end of my first term, my personal tutor encouraged me, saying my academic abilities had not disappeared the day I arrived in Cambridge! He described Cambridge as stratospheric – feeling that the level required of me was up in the stratosphere, whilst I was still on earth. This, apparently, was a normal feeling, and did not mean I had anything to fear. Encouraged, I refused to let myself believe that there was anything in my lectures that I could not understand (fellow Natural Scientists will immediately know from this that I did not take any physical science modules!).

I managed to achieve (academic) success at Cambridge. By the end of three years, I could write a reasonably good essay and could argue persuasively about climate change and conservation (I've tried it on my friends. Some of them are convinced). I had successfully combined rowing for my college and church activities with academic studies, and graduated with a 1st. I later found out that, averaged across all three years, I was the highest performing student in my college. I had already applied to study for a PhD at Cambridge, and now my hard work truly paid off. Despite my lack of experience in fieldwork, computer modelling, relevant statistics or the use of ArcGIS, I was accepted.

I loved my PhD. I was the happiest I had ever been, working with fantastic people at the top of the field, learning huge amounts and enjoying every second of it. Well, almost. Data entry never comes high on anyone's enjoyment list.

As part of my PhD, I went out to collect data on the vegetation cover of several lowland heaths around the UK. The sun was out almost every day for the three months I was out, and the bright yellow and deep green of the gorse contrasted beautifully with the clear blue skies. I watched red deer, fallow deer, sika deer and muntjacs (with the last two being non-native to the UK I would have been happier not to see them!). Blue butterflies, painted ladies and dragonflies would flash by in bright streaks of colour, or rest tantalisingly on heather, daring me to attempt a photograph. I caught glimpses of lizards, walked past sun-bathing adders, and stopped to let slow-worms slink across my path. It was, in all, an incredible time to be out and to enjoy a part of nature that, as one brought up in the north, I had never been able to appreciate before.

During a planned break over Easter, I was surprised to discover that even after several days spent reading chick-lit and sleeping, I was still very tired. I'm not usually a fan of chick-lit, preferring books with a bit more social insight, so in itself my reading chick-lit was a sign that something could be wrong. Disconcertingly, this continued all week. But my habits and attitudes were well engrained, and as I have never let myself do average quality work, I was not going to start slacking then. At the end of my holiday I duly went back to the fieldwork. It was a lonely time. I was still tired and was surprised that I could not talk myself into a better mentality. I expected the fieldwork to get easier, as I built up stamina and became used to so much outdoor work, but this did not happen. Instead, with each passing week, I grew more and more tired, developed stomach ulcers and struggled to eat. I found that I was sore when I woke up in the morning, but it wasn't stiffness that wears off during the day. Mild pain was now a constant presence.

More to my concern, I found that my brain seemed to be slowing down and losing its grip on simple tasks. It felt like an old computer, overloaded with files and concurrent programs, messed up by a few viruses and without much RAM. There wasn't the processing power I needed available to me any more. I have never been one to drink tea or coffee, but now I needed something to counteract my tiredness and prevent a decline in the quality of my work. I started taking caffeine tablets to keep myself alert, and also to combat the increasing desire to sit down and cry.

But with each passing day, the struggle to keep going was getting harder. Finally, break point came. I had to stop. It was the first time I had not completed a piece of work on time. It was also the first time I was not pleased with the quality of my work. I assumed that with a lot of rest over a couple of weeks I would recover, thinking that there was nothing more wrong with me than the customary tiredness felt by anyone engaged in fieldwork. When, a week after returning to Cambridge, I was still unwell, I went to see a GP. He diagnosed me as having post-viral fatigue, although I was unaware of any illness that might have triggered the fatigue and tested negative for Glandular Fever. He suggested that I take things a little easier over the next few weeks and sleep as much as I wanted.

My health continued to deteriorate. After consultation with a second GP and with my PhD supervisor, it was agreed that I would finish my first-year report and then take three months off. I wanted to be allowed to switch to a part-time programme, feeling that this would allow me to continue to work at the level my health permitted, but this was not permitted in my department. So, having handed in the first-year report (what I had been doing and planned to do in my PhD, to confirm my ability to complete a doctoral thesis in the next three years), I moved back in with my parents.

I decided to give myself a month completely off, no work at all, and then gradually re-introduce some work in order to be used to 40 hour weeks by the beginning of December. This was going okay, until I found that reading even a simple paper (I love reading, so for me this represented a gentle task to get used to work again) was like reading a paper from a different scientific discipline –

full of words of which I had not the slightest clue to their meaning. At the same time I became unable to walk around the house without leaning on walls, furniture and anything available in order to keep my balance and spread my weight a little more. I had to think consciously about everything I did – how to walk, how to grip, how to lift a glass of water to my mouth, how to chew and swallow. Loud noises and bright lights became unbearable, and my favourite 'activity' was to lie quietly in the dark, avoiding all sensory stimuli.

That shelved my plans to return to the PhD in December. I registered with a doctor nearer my parents and arranged to take another term off, from January to March. I started on anti-depressants and a host of other medications, all aimed at relieving the symptoms of ME (Myalgic Encephalopathy). The cause of ME is unknown, so doctors can only help sufferers by prescribing medication to relieve, as much as possible, the many symptoms, and by recommending a course of 'pacing' or Graded Exercise Therapy. Whilst G.E.T. and Cognitive Behavioural Therapy are what the current NICE guidelines for ME advise, these methods are not popular amongst the ME population and are condemned by many researchers.

My health continued to deteriorate. Realising how little I could do without making myself worse took a long time! I was constantly believing that I could do something, that it wouldn't make me worse, only to find that I was unable to get around my house, couldn't focus my eyes to read, and couldn't read a simple passage of prose without feeling after ten minutes as though I had just sat a 5-hour exam. I was too used to the mentality of a society that looks down on 'scroungers.' Eventually I gave in and admitted that my baseline activity was no activity at all. I had to build, very, very slowly, from there; I had to admit that I couldn't will myself better; I had to accept that, after spending so long believing in the importance of contributing to society, I now could now only take from the contributions of others.

Before Christmas I began to use a wheelchair to get out of the house. My brother was at home, earning money during his gap year to pay for a 6-month trip to South

Africa. He kept me entertained and well stocked-up with hugs. He also took me out for walks (or rolls, in my case), which was quite a sacrifice given we lived on a hill! He would run up the hill, trying each time to get a little further before running out of puff. On the way home, he would hold on to the handles of the wheelchair and lift his feet off the ground (don't try this at home. Wheelchair brakes are designed for remaining stationary, not for slowing or stopping a wheelchair). If we got a straight line down the centre of the lane, ensuring that we did not turn with the camber towards the walls down each side, we could pick up a lot of speed. On my brother's last day before flying to Johannesburg, we managed this perfectly, and when his feet made contact with the ground again to aid in braking, the impact was more than a little painful!

I had a major crash in January, following the exhaustion of Christmas. At the end of January, my parents bought me a dog to keep me company during the 6-7 hours of the day when they were both out at work. It was an unexpected decision, prompting many enquiries from friends curious to know why my dad had agreed to have an animal in the house again! It was also a great blessing, helping to lift my mood which by this point was very low. Rafiki (Swahili for friend), 6-months old at the time we got him, quickly settled in. He developed a strange tendency towards vegetarianism – he happily takes hyacinth flowers, oranges, apples, pears and bananas, and adores carrots and broccoli (which is toxic in large amounts. We try not to give it to him, but sometimes we forget and he takes it off the kitchen side whilst we are not looking. I'm working on teaching him better manners).

Towards the end of February, it became necessary for me to consider returning to my PhD (I was due to return at the beginning of April). My health was still very poor. I have various ways to measure my health. One is the state of my bedroom; generally a tidy person, a messy room is a sure sign that my mood is low. Jigsaws also are a useful measure; if I can complete a standard 500-1000 piece jigsaw in a single afternoon, I am fine; if it takes a month, then I am far from well! Sudokus are similarly informative. When I fail to solve a puzzle that is meant to be completed within the time to brew a cup of tea (or maybe to drink a cup of tea; I am never sure; but a short time anyway!) then something is seriously wrong. With these and other, more serious, assessments of my health, I made the decision to withdraw from my PhD. It was clear by this point that my health was not going to improve significantly any time soon, and any attempt to pick up work again was only a good idea if my aim was to make myself bed-bound.

This takes me to the present day. I continue to live with my parents, entirely supported them – and believe me, with the cost of physio every two-three weeks, trips to the doctor (half an hours drive, but worth it to get a doctor who understands both me and my condition), and non-prescription supplements, my maintenance is not a small sum of money! An attempt to claim Employment and Support Allowance before Christmas, in the hope that this would allow me, rather than my parents, to defray the cost of my healthcare, was turned down on the basis that I had never paid any National Insurance Contributions (at 22, having always been in education, how could I?). I used to walk 300m, and my ankles, shins, knees and thighs would all burn in complaint. As I send this book to print I can walk a fraction of that distance, once a day if I'm lucky. I feel sick from too much short-distance focussing, and my finger-tips hurt from the impact of typing. My throat is sore, a side-effect of my painkillers, and yet I am still in constant pain. I cannot wash my hair without the pressure hurting my scalp; I cannot sit in one position for more than a few minutes before aching muscles and joints demand a change. I find watching a film exhausting, and have to rest afterwards.

I am fed up of being useless, and often engage in activities that I know are too physically demanding, because if I did not then my mood would drop to worryingly depressed levels. It is not so much a balancing act between looking after myself physically and looking after myself emotionally, as alternating between the two in an attempt to prevent either from becoming too severe. I forget what I wanted to say (or right now, type, as has just happened) seconds after thinking of it; I forget words so completely that I do not even recollect that there is a suitable word to fit whatever it is I am trying to say; I confuse events that happened in dreams with reality.

And despite all the best efforts of my doctor, physio, therapist and parents, I am still unable to walk 300m. In fact, today that much was too far, and I had to stop several times. I still require seven different prescription medications and three supplements, a number far surpassed by many fellow ME sufferers. My mental faculties are far below what they were when I studied at Cambridge. I can just about cope with having a friend to visit – if I sleep afterwards. My life is planned around sleep. Everything I do, I have to consider how much energy it demands and how long I will need afterwards before having the energy to do something else. Having breakfast and getting showered and dressed count as activities that demand anywhere between thirty minutes and two hours rest afterwards. If I want a drink of water, I have to decide whether my thirst is worse than the added pain and tiredness that getting up, walking to the sink, reaching up to get a glass out of the cupboard, filling the glass and lifting it to my mouth will require. Things that most people count as things to do *before* starting the activities of the day, are things that to me *are* the activities of the day.

This is my reality. This is what I mean when I say I am tired, and that I ache. So yes, tiredness. We're all used to it, and we all get on with life despite it. We don't let it stop us from going to work, make us neglect the washing (or at least, not for too long!), or neglect to ensure the children get to school. We're quite used to getting on with the job, pulling ourselves together and not making a big fuss about it. But don't forget the reality faced by these people who claim they're 'too tired' to work. Try to understand why we – myself and my fellow ME/CFS sufferers - don't give ourselves a good talking to, quit moaning and do as your typical healthy person does – get a job, and have a life.

We are the people with Myalgic Encephalopathy and Chronic Fatigue Syndrome, the ones whose lives are dominated by persistent fatigue and aches and pains. The people you look at and wonder, 'What are they making so much fuss about? We all get tired, and most of us deal with it!' The people you see smiling and laughing, maybe even walking their child to school, leaving you asking yourself why someone so clearly fit and healthy is sponging off the state?

If you take the time to look and listen, you will find that we are not as healthy as you assumed. The fatigue we describe is nothing like you have ever experienced. The smiles on our faces are fixed in an attempt to forget and conceal, however briefly, the pain and exhaustion that are constantly with us. If we walk our children to school, it is because our concentration is too poor to drive safely, and there have been too many days already this term when we have been unable to get our children there.

As you consider this, consider also these quotes from similarly affected people, and ask yourself – are you working hard enough?

"Living with Fibromyalgia is something no-one can really understand unless they've gone through it. As well as the horrendous physical symptoms of 24/7 pain, exhaustion, insomnia etc; and taking 25 plus tablets a day, you have to deal with the guilt that it affects everyone who cares about you. I'd be ecstatic to feel 'a bit peaky.'" *Leanne, as quoted by Jason Reed, The Huffington Post, 27/1/12, in response to Rod Liddle (quoted above).*

"Like most ME/Fibro sufferers, I am overtly susceptible to negativity, so it is hastily lanced from my life like an infected boil. Take that as you will, Mr Liddle – and, as you giggle at the bar over your latest storm, I shall have to take my leave of absence to rest; funny that. The final irony is: ME/Fibro sufferers tend to be dedicated individuals who have pushed themselves to the limits of human endurance. Athletes, academics, and life's overachievers. And yet, we're labelled as lazy. So, the point is, with tongue firmly in cheek - if you haven't got ME/Fibro, then you've simply not tried hard enough." *Jason Reed, The Huffington Post, 27/1/12, in response to Rod Liddle.*

7

Colin's Story: Living with ME

I'm quite an expert in my condition. I've had it seven years. I know what most of the standard treatments are. I know what is just about okay for me to do and what makes me worse. I know I can't work right now because it would cause a serious deterioration in my health.

I'm not saying this just from a knowledge of myself and of my illness. I'm saying this because actually, as a qualified general nurse and psychiatric nurse with a psychology degree, I really know a bit about medical and mental matters as well. My wife is a GP, so she has some understanding of these things too.

So when I was told a year ago that I would be fit for work in three months' time from that date, I didn't understand. I'd been ill for seven years. If my recovery were a mere three months away, wouldn't I be one of the first to recognise that? Wouldn't my wife and my GP also have picked up on it? Why was a person with no specialist knowledge and no prior knowledge of me better able to make a judgment on my fitness for work? And yet this person had been permitted to take away the support we so desperately need since I became ill and unable to work.

I didn't choose this illness. I didn't choose to be dependent on government benefits, and certainly have not gone on benefits as a 'lifestyle choice.' I didn't choose to be unable to support my wife and children, the youngest of whom was four years old when I became chronically ill. I didn't choose to remain ill for seven years. I was simply a victim of life's unpredictable circumstances, and now also a victim of two successive governments that wished to restrict the payment of health-related benefits.

I invite you to walk through my life with me, to live with me for a short time, just as I am living with ME and have lived with ME for a long time.

I used to work as a general nurse and a psychiatric nurse. My wife, as a GP, had a more demanding job than I did. We had three children, between four and nine years old. If I had not become ill, we would have had no problem supporting our family entirely through our own work.

Previous to becoming ill, I was on the Parish Church Council of the local Anglican church which we all attended. I was also in the mission group and on the prayer rota. My wife and I loved the Bible and loved to study it, and we spent many weekends at Bible conferences. We were enthused, committed; in Christian parlance we were 'on fire.'

We were also decorating, or I was. I would come home, have a pint of beer, try to relax, and then start on decorating. Often I would go to bed at midnight and be up again at 6am for work. With three young children and a demanding job it was not a sensible lifestyle.

I was on the edge, and I knew it. We were older parents, and neither of our respective parents lived nearby to help out as we raised our children. I was being stretched, and stretched, and stretched. I developed mouth ulcers. I would drive to work feeling ill, have a couple of coffees on arrival, and push through regardless.

Before I became ill I was referred to a specialist. The consultant diagnosed me as having neck cancer, based on an ultrasound. A CAT scan was needed to get more detail, but the urgent referral was lost. My wife and I were tense: it was like living in a black cloud. We tried to hide it from the children; our youngest caught my expression in an unguarded moment and said, "Why do you look so sad, Daddy?" We didn't know what was before us.

The urgent referral was sent again. I had the scan. It was clear; I did not have cancer.

Exactly one month after finding out I was cancer-free, I was up all night with our four-year-old who was being sick. My wife had more responsibility in her job than I did, so the childcare fell to me. At work, I had a small lunch (my wife had suggested I diet), and kept going through the tiredness, staring at a computer screen all afternoon.

A blinding headache came on; fine one second, head splitting open the next. The ache went throughout my body and I had to rush to the loo. I felt wrecked, systemically; I knew I was broken. I somehow managed to drive home but returned to work late that afternoon as I had tasks to do. That evening I left work for the last time for a year. Over that year I had some improvement and a gastroenterologist check-up, then attempted a return to work in 2006 to try to keep my job. I tried a short morning walk before the day's work and I pushed myself beyond my limits. I 'worked' for a week and a half, getting more and more fatigued, before coming to a halt. Soon after, I took my children on a bike ride with a visiting friend. Unexpectedly I cycled for much further than I had planned. I was so ill that I 'crashed' catastrophically and was housebound for two years after that.

By this time I qualified for higher rate Disability Living Allowance. I applied for Incapacity Benefit, the precursor to Employment and Support Allowance. Waiting for my medical assessment, I lay down in the waiting room. I was so ill that I literally could not have remained seated in the chairs provided. I was awarded IB. Since then, I have had questionnaires and telephone assessments every year to check whether or not I continued to deserve IB. I was also eligible for DLA, although it took me a year to get round to applying for it.

I could barely walk. My wife had hurt her back with lifting things, so she couldn't get a wheelchair in and out of our car, and I made do. I seriously considered crawling on the pavement when I needed to get to a bank or any task that needed me rather than my wife. But crawling on pavements is not socially acceptable, and certainly would never be a suitable compromise when it was raining. I did sit down during queues, such as at the building society; I didn't mind what people thought of me.

I used to play games of Solitaire and Patience, over and over. My wife thought it was nonsensical; I was putting a strain on my physical and mental abilities that would make me worse. But I needed to do something, and this kept me occupied. It is difficult to explain to someone who has not personally experienced ME, but there is a need to keep some level of activity going even though it exhausts you; it's something to distract the mind from the pain and fatigue of the current situation.

My wife used to give me instructions for dinner, but I would forget them. I couldn't put names to things and would leave sentences uncompleted. My wife thought it was just my personality; perhaps I was just scatty. Even she, as my wife and a GP with interest in ME, did not understand my condition and its effect on me.

A friend sent me an e-mail from the Hilton Health Club which led to my having a free trial. I discovered that one of the best things I could do was lie in the sauna or steam room, and if I felt up to it I would lie in the pool afterwards. It was expensive, but it was the only thing that in any way helped. For two years I was unable to stand to shower and needed to sit on a plastic chair.

I had a period of therapy. I was told to 'project manage.' What these people didn't realise was that I already 'project managed.' I have to plan every part of my day. If I need to get something from upstairs, I have to plan what to do before and after that, to be adequately rested and not make myself worse. For example it would take me a whole week to empty all the bins in the house, a tiny step at a time, then put the wheelie-bin out. I didn't need more project managing, and lack of it was neither the cause nor a continuing factor in my illness.

Specialised services for ME only made me worse. I was too ill to attend any groups. I preferred to surround myself with normality and associate with largely healthy people. I didn't want to become trapped into a sickness lifestyle.

Useful advice was rare. My GP could offer me medication to treat the various symptoms, but could do nothing about the underlying cause of my illness. My referral to a specialist was not useful either. The only advice offered was the 'project managing' type advice which I did not need to be told to do. My illness is not psychological, so psychological help is only of limited value. Experienced medics were unable to offer any better advice. I preferred to focus on God and the hope that He offers.

In November 2011 it was my turn to be reassessed for the new benefit, Employment and Support Allowance. By that time I had 6 years' experience of my illness. I knew far more about it than most GPs, nurses or physiotherapists. I knew I could not work.

I had not received any advice about the application process for ESA, and was therefore unprepared for the interview. I have since found out that it is advisory to give information on what you can do reliably and repeatably which takes into account your worst days. But I was over-optimistic in my abilities as I only focussed on my good days. But with the government's emphasis on fraud (despite fraud levels being very low) and rhetoric of benefit scroungers, there is often a reluctance amongst disabled people to admit just how difficult things are. Certainly I was afraid to say I could not walk, in case an emergency arose that required me to walk and someone saw me. Although this would make me even more ill, onlookers only see the walking, and not its consequences. So in my assessment, I talked about what happens in an ideal situation, rather than on a bad day or on average over a few weeks or months.

As a consequence of my overly-positive slant on my illness, I was informed that I would be fit for work in three months.

The stress this judgment caused me was immense. Up to that point I had seen a slight improvement in my condition. Things that used to exhaust me hugely now only exhausted me slightly. I could manage a little bit more. Since that decision, however, I have not had any more improvement, however slight, in my health.

The judgment made me feel that the government were not listening to me. Despite being very ill, and very far from able to work, someone under government guidelines and laws had decided I was fit for work. It was as though everything I knew about myself was irrelevant and wrong; what mattered was someone else's opinion. I was officially 'well,' so how could I explain to others that, despite this government's decision, I was in fact ill?

I appealed the decision. I had to – three months after the decision I was still far away from the health required to sustain work. The decision to appeal had to be made within one month. Knowing myself and my illness as I did, I felt no hesitation.

The original decision had noted my limited physical ability, but not my fatigue, the cumulative effect of any activity, or the impact this had on my thinking and cognitive abilities. No consideration was given to the variability of my illness, making my ability to carry out any activity unreliable.[136]

I explained that my muscles were 'under tension' if I overdid things. I meant that my muscles were tight and painful; the pain and constant tension caused me extra fatigue and further reduced my ability to carry out any activity. I was interpreted to mean that I was stressed. I explained that I have nominal dysphasia (I forget words for things), but then my recollection of the correct term may have suggested otherwise to the assessor. I used to be on higher rate DLA (unable or virtually unable to walk), but explained that at a recent Christian camp I had been able to walk to the toilets and back, around 100m. This was submitted with the strong proviso that I would spend all the rest of the time lying in my tent. The information was taken to mean that I could walk 100m, despite this not being what I meant; I thought I had made it clear that 100m was the most I could do, if it was also the only thing I did.

The mismatch between my language and the assessor's meant that the assessor's report and conclusions were not accurately based on my reality. The assessment needs to be conducted in language that both the patient and the assessor understand. This is particularly important given some patients' reluctance to discuss their problems in the necessary detail, or in a realistic light.

---

[136] A person must be able to carry out an activity reliably to be considered as able to do it.

The questions I was asked had no context and bore little relation to any work place. They failed to capture what my condition is and how it affects me. I drove to the assessment, but parking was an issue. I still cannot walk far, and the ticket machine was not near the entrance of the assessment centre, so I had to stop by the machine to get a ticket, and then go back to park near the entrance. This was not flagged up to the job centre. The whole assessment was very short, around 20-30 minutes, and failed to probe into what limitations my illness has given me.

I knew far more about ME than my assessor did, and it was frustrating to be asked questions that were not relevant to ME. I knew what I could and could not do, but was dependent on the judgement of a person who had no prior knowledge of me, and less knowledge of ME than I did.

After my appeal I was put into the Work Related Activity Group for ESA. This meant that whilst I was recognised as unable to work, I was expected to be able to undertake activity that in some way relates to work. This meant getting to the Jobcentre when required. As I could now, if well rested, usually (although not always) walk about 50m, I no longer had a Blue Badge. I therefore could not park in the disabled spots close to the entrance. After my first experience, I always asked my wife to drive me there and drop me off near the entrance.

The first interview I had was a farce. The Jobcentre had only six metered spaces, and I arrived 30 minutes early in order to ensure I could have one. I went over to the ticket machine to get a 2-hour ticket, but the maximum wait was one hour. This was no use to me. There needed to be more spaces, and there needed to be longer waits allowed.

I had rung up in advance to find out what the parking arrangements were. I was told that I would be reimbursed for the cost of the ticket. When I spoke to the reception staff on the day, however, I was told that I could not be reimbursed. Reimbursements were only for those who came on the bus – something I was too ill to do.

In the building, I asked for a toilet but was informed that none were available and I would have to go to

Debenhams. This being too far for me, I had to ignore it and continue to the room where I was to present my case to an ESA officer. This was at the top of the building and at the other end. Having got there I was told where a toilet was, and was led back along the building, down the lift and along through the ground floor past security to reach the toilet. I then had to go back to the ESA desk for the interview.

Within ten minutes I was exhausted and unwell. The exertion of the walking coupled with the pressure I was under just from having to attend made me feel very faint. I could barely stand and I couldn't read. I suggested that I had a telephone interview in the afternoon, to allow me to recover, but this was refused. I therefore had to ask for the interview to end because of poor health. I signed a form, but I don't know what it said because I was too exhausted and ill to be able to focus on reading.

This interview occurred in June 2012, eight months after my assessment for ESA and five months after I was supposed to be well enough to be in work. I was furious afterwards; angry and upset that the DWP's staff and out-sourced staff were allowed to impose decisions on me that endangered my health. The next day I was completely bed-bound and sick. It took me two weeks to recover enough to be able to write a short letter of complaint explaining my experience.

I was sent to a session on enterprise. This was shorter. It was also unhelpful. I remember being recommended to spend time buying and selling items on E-bay. But if it were that simple, wouldn't everyone be doing it? Enterprises usually fail, and are unlikely to be unusually successful for people whose health renders them incapable of work, however capable of 'work related activity.'

I was asked what I do at home. I said that I do the laundry. With my wife and eldest daughter both now unwell, we all have to help out regardless of the risk this poses to our health. I help out by doing the laundry, because it is something that can be done very slowly and intermittently I can sit down and rest part way through.

However this takes up so much energy that it often makes me unwell.

It was suggested to me that I carry out laundry for elderly people, as a way back into work. This suggestion showed a complete lack of comprehension on the part of the Jobcentre staff concerned. I can manage the laundry precisely because it is an event that does not occur every day, and because I can do it slowly. Neither of these things would be true if I were to do other people's laundry as well as our own; and where would we hang it all to dry? We would probably struggle to pay the electricity for large numbers of washes.

My next session with the WRAG was on the state of the labour market. In a recession, it's pretty bad. There aren't many jobs even for people with several years of recent experience. There's even less work available for people who cannot even move the distance from a car parking space to a Jobcentre entrance. It wasn't useful – I was a graduate with a successful job seven years ago; I'm not someone with no understanding of jobs. The session was also far too long for someone suffering from an illness that causes pain and fatigue, and for which the result of slight overexertion is increased pain and fatigue for several weeks.

I have now been referred to a specialist ME centre. I hope that this specialist will be able to put my mind at rest and confirm that, despite what this government thinks, I am not well enough to be either in work or considering a return to work.

8

Danni's Story: Unseen Pain

There was once a girl. She had a disability, but nobody knew, because nobody could see. She wasn't in a wheelchair, she didn't use crutches, but she knew unbearable pain, isolation, depression; she knew what it felt like to get bad news constantly. That girl was me, and this is my story.

I was born with spina bifida. When I was born paediatricians believed it was just absence of skin over my spine. I wasn't diagnosed until I was 18months old, after several invasive tests. Apart from some incontinence when I was younger, and some slight difficulty with clumsiness as a five year old, it affected me very little. Indeed, I wasn't even aware of the words 'spina bifida;' just two words, but ones that were soon to taint who I was.

At the age of nine, my spinal cord twisted and caused nerve damage to my bladder, bowel and left leg. An operation to untether the spinal cord was carried out to stop any more damage, but it was too late. Over the next few months, I became incontinent and severely constipated. Test after test was performed; painful, intrusive, humiliating. I won't discuss all that went on, there isn't time, but by the age of eighteen I had had multiple surgeries, nearly every one of which was unsuccessful. I was left with terrible scars, both colostomy and urostomy bags, and I was extremely emotionally traumatised. By the time I was nineteen I was seeing a trauma psychologist for PTSD.

Life was hard for my parents as well as for me. In my first year at secondary school I missed more than 80% of classes and was falling badly behind. The state education was not good enough, and my frequent visits to hospital were interrupting even that, so my father left his job to educate me himself. This was a big life change for him, and the drop in our families' income added more stress to the already present emotional difficulties of having a severely sick child. Throughout those awful years my parents were my rock. They held me up, fought for the best healthcare for me and advocated on my behalf to the doctors, whom I would not speak to, having been traumatised by the surgeries and tests they had carried out.

After I had the urostomy formed in 2005, I believed that that would be an end to any more surgery; after all, surely they could do no more to me. I couldn't bear the thought that in the future there would be more tests, more intrusions into my life, more pain and more surgery. It had interrupted my education and now I badly wanted the space to have a steady job. I wanted to be a reliable worker, able to turn up on time and provide decent work; someone who would be viewed by an employer as an asset and not a financial drain.

But it was not the end. My right kidney began to swell up, and I fought kidney infections monthly. I was exhausted, in pain, could barely get out of bed sometimes. My body felt beaten and bruised, it hurt sometimes to breathe. I was fighting to continue in my job, working as a receptionist at a hotel. It was only twelve hours a week and even that was a struggle, but I was determined not to be defeated by my health. I was set on proving that I could be a valuable member of staff worth her wages (and sick pay).

Eventually, after enormous effort by my GP and my parents, we managed to persuade the local Primary Care Trust (PCT) to give me a four-week course of intra-venous antibiotics. This cost £2000 a week, hence the wrestle with the PCT, but it dealt effectively with the constant kidney infections. For a whole year I was infection-free. My energy came back, albeit very slowly, and in 2008 I managed to complete a years' worth of full time study, earning a foundation degree in Theology.

However, the constant infections had left their mark, and I had Chronic Nephritis, a condition in which the nephrons of the kidneys are inflamed. This caused such severe chronic pain that I ended up on morphine patches.

The painkillers caused more problems. I slept most days and lay awake all night; I couldn't think clearly and was chronically constipated. After six months of this, I decided I would rather cope with the pain, than live in this hell for the rest of my life. I came off the morphine cold turkey. I was only twenty-two. The experience was so hideous that I determined to never take morphine long term again.

Once I came off the patches, I found that the pain had reduced a bit, enough to live a relatively normal life at least. I got a job at Starbucks, working between twenty and twenty-five hours a week. I become coffee master and district coffee master, and started travelling around the country training other baristas. Life was looking up.

But then (I hate the word 'but') I developed a kidney infection. This rapidly turned into septicaemia, and I was rushed into hospital. As I began to recover, the old pain returned. My manager was very sympathetic and reduced my hours to sixteen to twenty per week. I found I could manage as long as I rested in between times. I felt so frustrated; I'd worked so hard at being healthy and keeping well and still my body thwarted me. I wanted to be a good employee but my body was not cooperating.

In early 2010, my bowel began to play up. Previously it had been only a minor worry – as minor as a colostomy can be. Now my colostomy stopped working for weeks at a time, I felt constantly sick and very skanky, a feeling that only comes with a full bowel. I also felt very fragile emotionally; things seemed to be falling apart on all sides. I couldn't control my health; I couldn't control my work; I couldn't control my life; and I was becoming ever less employable.

I requested some psychological help. Before this could be implemented by my GP I had an operation to correct a blockage in my bowel. This was major surgery that further disfigured my abdomen, already scarred from my previous operations. My recovery from this surgery was somewhat shaky. I developed an ileus, which occurs when the entire bowel paralyses so that food no longer passes through. I was vomiting my body weight, and couldn't even take fluids. The medical technique for dealing with an ileus is the wonderful treatment called 'drip and suck', which meant that I was given intra-venous fluids and had a nasogastric tube up my nose to drain fluid out of my stomach into a bag. This very unpleasant procedure was performed four times, before the medical team decided that they couldn't put a tube down my nose as I kept gagging and vomiting. After five days in hospital, my bowel finally decided to work and I went home, a stone lighter than when I went in (who needs diets, an ileus works just as well).

Twenty-four hours later I developed septicaemia from a kidney infection and ended up in the resuscitation ward. This was a terrible ordeal and I believed I was going to die. I had very little strength to fight an infection. Somehow I managed, and after another six days in hospital I went home, having lost another stone, and looking somewhat like a pixie.

By this time, my manager was beginning to become concerned with my ability to work, and I had to return to work early in order to keep my job. I also had to have an assessment done at work to decide whether or not I should be working there. Fortunately for me (from a work perspective), I passed and returned to work for twenty hours a week. Six months after my surgery, I was feeling very fit and considered myself to be doing quite well.

I loved my work at Starbucks and despite my poor and intermittent health, was doing well career-wise. Sadly their working hours weren't flexible enough for me, as I often had very bad days. These were unpredictable, so there was no way to plan work around them. I had a personal policy of always going to work if I were not in hospital, but this was not good for my health. I left Starbucks to work for a medical agency, which gave me more flexible hours. I could work more on good days and less on bad days, thus fitting my work around my health as much as possible. I had been working with them only five months when I developed an infection resistant to most antibiotics. The infection kept flaring up and I ended up in hospital three times in one month – not good for my health, and not good from the employer's perspective either.

After several tests, the doctors found that my right kidney wasn't draining, and so they inserted an artificial drain, the nephrostomy. This is a tube that starts in the kidney and comes out of one's back to drain into a bag. They are ugly, restrictive and often painful. The drain is usually inserted under local anaesthetic and sedation. A friend of mine who had previously had a nephrostomy told me afterwards that it was the most painful and traumatic thing he had ever experienced. He hadn't told me before because he didn't want to make me scared. However, the pain was so bad that I instinctively got up from the operating table and fought the sedatives (I like to think that this says something about my fighting spirit, but actually I think people probably just thought I was being awkward), so I had the procedure done under general anaesthetic instead.

Having a nephrostomy restricts many movements. One cannot bend over, pick up anything above 1kg or engage in sport. Clothing has to be loose, to ensure that the opening of the catheter does not get caught and pulled out of place. I could not return to work, and so I had to apply for Employment Support Allowance. I was distressed by this as I had always tried so hard to stay in employment. I did not want to give in or admit that I could not work. I firmly believe I should work to support myself and will go in to work even at times when most people would have taken sick leave days before.

The problems kept coming. The nephrostomy repeatedly became blocked, and so I had to keep going to casualty to have it cleared. I was rushed into casualty with renal colic, one of the worst pains I have ever had, and ended up on morphine and gas and air. I got another resistant infection, and spent a week in hospital. My veins were in such poor state by then from repeated IV lines that I had to have a long line inserted into one of the bigger veins. That line stayed in for a month whilst I was receiving treatment.

Whilst all this was going on, the doctors discovered that I had a blocked ureter, and that they needed to operate. This was not a simple procedure, so I had to be transferred to a specialist centre, two hundred miles away from where I lived. Needless to say, my mother and I made quite a few road trips. These were costly, time consuming, and in an emergency, a 200 mile trip isn't very feasible. I had several more tests up in Manchester, to confirm the diagnosis, and I had to have a new nephrostomy inserted as each one lasts only six months. More surgery followed just after my twenty-fifth birthday. Following on from this I had another life-threatening bout of septicaemia, which landed me in hospital on Christmas Day.

My recovery from the surgery was very slow, the pain and exhaustion overwhelmed me months afterwards, and the infections just kept coming. After several more tests, some very painful, my consultant informed me that the surgery had not made any difference to the drainage of the kidney. The kidney was even more swollen from the back-up of fluid as it failed to drain. My previous diagnosis of a blocked ureter was incorrect. I had no anatomical problems that could be corrected by surgery. Instead I had chronic kidney disease. This is untreatable.

The news was devastating. For so many years I had had hope that each surgery would be the last one, the one to solve all my problems. Each one I expected would take away the pain; stop the recurrent infections; allow my kidney to drain correctly. Instead, after years of trauma, I found out that much of it may have been useless. I was left scarred emotionally and physically. I will never spend a year pain free; I will never get rid of the kidney infections that repeatedly could turn septic and kill me; I will never be a reliable worker because I can never predict when I will be in hospital on the resuscitation ward or sedated by morphine in an attempt to cope with the pain. Pain and sickness frighten me far worse than an early death; I have no death-wish, but death is preferable to a long life of chronic pain. I am still only 25.

My doctor referred me to the pain team, a move that in my mind at least is a last resort. What I already knew was confirmed by the Pain Clinic consultant - there are no magical drugs that take away pain. Paracetamol is not very effective unless it is administered intravenously, which is not possible at home. I cannot take Ibuprofen and other

NSAIDS. Tricyclic antidepressants such as amitriptyline and anti-epileptics such as gabapentin give me terrible hallucinations. The only painkillers that the team could recommend (morphine and codeine) were the ones I already take, and already hate because of the side-effects. I was offered psychological help but I had already received two years of therapy, and the doctor said I would only be going over techniques I had already learnt.

And so, to summarize, I have a colostomy, urostomy and a non-draining right kidney, with chronic pain and infections that can lay me up at any time, for any length of time. I can never predict the timing, duration, quality or quantity of work that I can do on any given day.

I want to get back to work as soon as possible, but with more operations likely in the not too distant future, the unreliability of attendance due to my pain and infections, and the lack of qualifications because of the amount of interrupted study I have had, who exactly will employ me?

9

Elan's Story: One Fit at a Time

I've had epilepsy since birth. My parents didn't know what was wrong with me for a long time. I have cerebral palsy too, so the epilepsy wasn't diagnosed until I was four or five. It doesn't really bother me – it's part of who I am – but it is still scary at times.

School was always difficult for me. Because of my fits I experienced quite a bit of bullying. Children don't always understand epilepsy. I was seen as weird because of it, and in the way of children this was seen as a reason to exclude me. I learnt to stand up for myself and would get into fights; not the best way to respond from a grown-up's perspective, but I only knew that I had to defend myself. The bullying wouldn't go away by my ignoring it.

I had been put on carbamazepine when I was first diagnosed. I took it in its liquid form. The drug was reasonably effective and I even went a year and a half without any seizures. I was hugely pleased by this. I thought that at last I would be able to act like any other normal teenager. I would no longer have to worry about always being able to find a safe place to have a fit if one came on.

That was in my early teens, but in the next few years the epilepsy changed. I didn't know at the time, but epilepsy often manifests itself differently in adults compared to children. When I was 16 I had a mega fit. I collapsed and was unconscious for four hours.

After that collapse I had to go back on the meds. I started a second line of meds as well, because the epilepsy was now more difficult to control. It was a stressful time. I was trying to adjust to new medication and the side-effects; anti-epileptics are very strong drugs and can have some nasty effects on the body. The fits had started up again after the mega-fit so now I was dealing with all the normal difficulties of teenage years whilst re-adjusting to the limitations that unpredictable fits put on one's life.

My second line of meds didn't work. I knew it wasn't working, but no-one was listening to me. I had to battle on for several years before my doctors accepted what I was saying. All that time I was having more and more fits, ending up by averaging one or two a fortnight. Finally I was listened to and I stopped taking that drug, and started on a third to complement the first drug that I was still taking.

I had a fit once on the way to London. I was making my way there alone. Sometimes I do that – I decide that today I am not going to let the epilepsy dictate what I do. I won't let it dictate my life. This was one of those days.

The fit came on whilst I was walking down a street. General seizures are often preceded by partial seizures, also known as auras. Partial seizures are when only part of the brain is affected. Simple partial seizures can manifest as a change in perception – things may look, smell, feel, taste or sound different to normal. Or there may be intense emotion or feeling of déjà vu. There may also be twitching, feelings of pins and needles, or stiffness down one side of the body. These give the person warning that a general seizure is coming.

The aura gave me time to look for somewhere safe to have a fit. This was the middle of a public road, so such places weren't obviously available. I certainly couldn't find any. The fit came on whilst I was still outside, on the street, with all the public around.

Usually after a fit I go home to lie down. I am always exhausted afterwards and can easily sleep all day. This occasion I was still feeling stubborn, so didn't go home. I continued on, getting a taxi to the train station, going to the gig, staying out till 4am. It's not always the most sensible thing to do as regards to my physical health, but sometimes it is necessary for my mental health that I briefly behave like a normal person and live as though my epilepsy does not exist.

Another fit came on just after I had been to a gig. I had left the building and was walking home. As the aura came, my first thought was to get somewhere safe. Having fits outside is dangerous, particularly near roads. Most of my fits are the atonic-clonic type, which means that my body relaxes and contracts in turn. This is the type most people think of when someone talks about epilepsy. Because of the relaxation, I will fall and when I am outside there is the possibility that I will fall into the road.

I could only think to go back to the gig. I didn't know where else would be a safe place to go. With the fit coming on, I ran back across two main roads and collapsed as I got through the door to the gig. The bouncers at first thought I was drunk, and were about to throw me out. That's quite common, as people don't always understand fitting or why I shake. But one of the bouncers realised it was epilepsy, so they looked after me whilst the fit wore itself out.

Most of the time I can manage the epilepsy. My meds have got it largely under control, so I don't have as many fits now as I used to. I know I have to keep an eye on what I drink, as alcohol can trigger my fits. So I don't drink as much now – at least it's cheaper that way! And I tend to stay with friends who know about my epilepsy. That way I can be kept safe when a fit occurs. They know I will be alright in a minute and aren't bothered by it.

Lack of sleep increases the likelihood of fits as well. I have to make sure I get enough sleep. My medication makes me very sleepy, so I never lack motivation! It can be really difficult at work sometimes, when my whole body wants so much to sleep. When I first started one of my medications, I was given a very high dose. It made me so exhausted it was like my brain and body were no longer connected. That was pretty horrible.

The fits are scary when they happen. The rest of the time I'm fine with it and don't really remember that I have epilepsy. But when the fits come, then I remember. I can injure myself quite badly. I try to get indoors, although then there is less space and I can end up with bruises or hit my head against a wall or furniture.

I'm very dependent on the good will of my employer and colleagues. I have to take the day off after a fit so that I can recover. I can get migraines as well; often I won't mention it and will work through but I can't always do that. It is important that my employer understands this and doesn't get at all annoyed or upset with how many sick days I have to have. My epilepsy means the work I do has to be one where frequent and unpredictable sick days is not going to cause any problems, like missing a meeting or an important deadline.

Understanding from my colleagues is also a big factor influencing what work I can do. It would be really difficult if they disapproved or got upset by my taking time off; any bad feeling towards me from my colleagues if they thought I were a 'slacker,' or faking it in order to get days off would make my work life awkward. I am lucky to have very good colleagues.

The nature of my work means it is common to have a high turnover of staff. This is the most difficult part for me. When people who know and accept me and my epilepsy leave, I have to go through the whole process of explaining about it with the new member of staff. I don't mind talking about it but other people sometimes find it difficult at first.

I don't try to make an issue out of it. It isn't an issue for me; most of the time I hardly think about it. I have to carry out certain precautions, like avoiding crowds, checking new places for somewhere safe if a fit comes on and being around people who know me. Fits come on within a couple of minutes so I have to know where to go quickly, the best way out of a crowd. But most of the time until a fit comes on I tend to forget about it. This can make explaining things a bit trickier as I don't hold the details of what it is like at the forefront of my mind; sometimes I have to think quite hard before I can explain properly to new people.

I've never had any trouble getting benefits. My mum has always helped me fill out the forms. I get the care component of DLA, but worry that when the changes come I won't get anything. I'll probably have to have a medical test.

It can be very difficult; I spend most of my time trying to manage my epilepsy so it has as small an influence on my life as I can make it, but then in a medical I suddenly have to be able to explain to a stranger how big it actually is. Sometimes it's like I have to prove to them that I am disabled, because they'd rather say that I'm not really that disabled. I try not to live like it, but the truth is epilepsy is disabling.

The epilepsy means I cannot drive. It also means I have to have continuous care, because a fit could come on at any time. It limits the work I can do, not just because there is some work that would be dangerous for an epileptic but also because some more high-pressured jobs wouldn't be suitable for someone who cannot reliably work. I hope with the government's changes I will still be recognised as needing the care that I do need, but I'm not confident of it.

10

Fin's Story: An Unseen World

I wasn't born blind. That makes me lucky in some ways. I know what colour is, and what things look like. I don't have any specific memories though. I was too young when my eyes were taken out.

I was born with the hereditary disease retinoblastoma bilateral. It meant I developed cancer in both of my eyes whilst I was a baby. The doctors tried to treat it but were unsuccessful. After 18 months, when I was two years old, they operated to remove both my eyes. I now have false eyes, which are so realistic that despite my white stick many people do not believe I am blind.

Primary and secondary school education wasn't a problem for me, despite being blind. I didn't notice much difference between myself and the other, sighted children. I had dedicated support workers who were given the subject material in advance of the lesson. They used this to prepare material that was accessible to me. There was a lot of effort put in to supporting me at school. Without this effort, I could not have had access to an education equal to the general education of a sighted child. It is very important that this level of support is given to all impaired children, whether the impairment is visual or otherwise.

What was difficult for me was the attitudes of other people and how they acted. I was often told that I should not play with the other children; I should sit on a bench throughout break time. The adults were scared that I would get hurt or lost. I did not accept that – I was not going to sit for their convenience! So I would go off and play, quite happily and without causing or being caught up in any problems.

The first difficulties I had with education came during my A-levels. I had determined to sit for A-levels because I knew it would be near to impossible for me to get a job without them. Most of my teachers were very good and would hand the material to my support workers in advance, so that it would be prepared for me. But there was one particular teacher who routinely failed to do this; as a result I struggled hugely in that subject. My parents recognised this and paid for a private tutor to help me in that subject.

My education was therefore more costly than for the average child. I had to have special staff to assist me, paid for by the state, and I had to have a private tutor, paid for by my parents.

University was the first time when many of the difficulties of being blind became apparent. Up till then, provision by the state and my parents had ensured I was not greatly disabled by my impairment. At university, I experienced the first indications of just how disabling being blind is when society and institutions have not adapted to the needs of blind people.

I had applied to read Maths. I already knew how to use a program for the blind, LaTeX, that translates Maths into spoken English. The only way I could communicate in Maths was through this programme. It was quite daunting to use. The fraction ½ would have to be written as /frac(1)(2) – clumsy and awkward.

Maths wise, I coped with my first year. It was the social and access part that was difficult. Not having any eyes meant that my brain had no way of picking up on the change from light to dark each evening. This meant that a crucial hormone involved in sleep, melatonin, was not produced in my body. Each night I took melatonin tablets which enabled me to get to sleep. However if I woke up during the night I could not get back to sleep. Because of this, I had asked to be given accommodation in a quiet hall to ensure that I would not get woken during the night.

I was given a room in one of the noisiest halls. Each night, students would come back after midnight having spent an evening on the town. They were noisy, disruptive and often played loud music. I complained, and security then insisted that the students did not continue to make noise, but their coming in was still noisy and would still wake me up.

I began to suffer hugely from sleep deprivation, because so many nights I would be woken in the very early morning and be unable to sleep again for the rest of the night. There was nothing I could do to increase the amount of sleep I was getting. Eventually I got a doctor's note and agreed to move out of hall. The university offered me the option to move into what was ostensibly a quiet hall. I chose instead to move in with a family I knew from church. I needed a guarantee that I would be able to sleep, not just a hope.

I didn't make any friends during my first year. I don't know whether this is because I am blind or is just me, but I have always struggled to make friends. The people I associated with were happy to include me in their circle but never spoke to me. Many times I have thought I had become friends with someone, only to find that any special effort or help they offered was because I was blind, not because I was a friend. It has been difficult to find that so many people relate to me as blind, not as a person.

Getting around was also interesting. It has always been horribly difficult. Having a guide dog would be impractical for me, and unfair on the dog because I would not be able to give it the exercise and the interest that it would need. I use a white stick to get around, which helps identify unexpected objects or uneven surfaces on pavements, but isn't perfect. In unfamiliar places I always need someone with me. Even in familiar places I need a sighted person around, even if it is just knowing that I am in a place with members of the public, to make sure that I am safe.

To get to my lectures I had to cross a busy road. I crossed this road twice a day throughout my time at university. In all that time, I received only three offers of help.

At the crossing point there was an island in the road. But this was placed near a bend on one side and just after a hill on the other. I couldn't hear cars coming from one side until they had topped the hill, and from the other side until they were around the bend. I often would wait for over five minutes, listening hard for a gap in the traffic. Sometimes I would miss one, not realising until the gap was gone, and then I would have to wait another five times.

Sometimes I would walk down the road to a place where there was no island. But here there were no bends or hills, so I could hear when gaps occurred and then run for it. It wasn't a particularly safe way to cross, but I didn't always have much choice.

The first time I was helped across, the lady came up to me very tentatively and asked if I would like help. I was very grateful. The second time it was the same lady.

She said, "Oh, I helped you before, would you like help again?"

"Yes, yes please," I replied.

The third time it was a jogger who helped me. He had run past, seen that I missed an opportunity to cross, and come back to help me.

Those were the only times.

Sometimes I would hear people walk past and I would ask them for help, but they walked on. It was a noisy and busy road, so perhaps they didn't hear.

Second year at university was terrible. For the first time I hugely struggled, and there was inadequate support for me. I was disabled by the lack of provision. I withdrew from the course after my exams, before I even had the results, because I knew I had failed. My best mark on the maths papers was 11%. There was one piece of group work about communicating in maths. I contributed to the communication part of it and left the maths to the others. We got 63% on that piece.

I did manage to make a couple of friends though. A young lady who attended my lectures and had seen me walking there and back came up to me and offered to walk with me. Later she introduced me to one of her friends. We started to walk to lectures together as well as back, and sometimes met up for meals. They were the first, and only, friends I made at university.

Having left university I had to look for a job. I hadn't managed to get my degree, so graduate jobs were out. What surprised me was the near impossibility of getting a job with just A-levels. I had no experience, no degree, and the extra difficulties of being blind. No-one wanted me.

I have started working at a local café. Everything is priced very cheaply and people on low incomes are encouraged to come and make use of the toddlers group that is available. In this way the café workers and volunteers are able to meet people who are in need of support and build relationships with them. The café is linked to the local food bank, so can help coordinate meetings between people in need of support and the people who offer it.

I love working there. I am able to help, to do something that contributes to the wellbeing of other people. Mostly I do the washing up but I do also get to chat with some of the people who come. Doing the washing up means people who can do things like serving and waitressing are freed up for that. I work at the toddler group as well. My first time, the toddlers were making gingerbread men. I helped one young boy to roll out the dough and cut it into shape with the cutter, which was fine, but stopping him from eating each cut out dough was more challenging!

I continue to look for jobs. I'm looking for reception or cleaning work. I can clean, although it is slower for me than for other people. I have to do it very methodically to make sure that everything is covered, and feel whether things are clean or not. It is important that people don't move things around, otherwise they become trip hazards to me. But with so many cleaning jobs putting a premium on speed, I'm unlikely to find any employer who would take me.

I don't have any experience in reception work either. I can use computers with software like Dolphin, Jaws or Screenreader to assist me. Access to Work would pay for the technology I needed to carry out a job if I were offered a position. I still wouldn't be able to read or sort post though, and it would take me longer than a sighted person to get up to a decent speed in the tasks required. Some programs are still very difficult – slideshow programs are a nightmare, and I lack all the visual cues for how to do even simple operations. All these things don't make me look like a good prospective employee. The government needs to invest a lot more in making the workplace accessible before I will have the same opportunities as a non-impaired person.

I would like to be a maths tutor. Group situations are difficult for me because I have to concentrate very hard to separate all the sounds. But I could do one-on-one teaching. If the pupil read his work back to me I could check if the answer and the intervening computations were correct. If the pupil can't explain his reasoning, then I know that there is a gap in his understanding. It will take me a while though to be able to get any sort of income from this kind of work.

Being blind undoubtedly reduces the number of jobs I can do. Anything that involves reading from a physical page, writing by hand or driving is completely ruled out. I can't use a physical diary, for example, although I could use one that is computer-based. I can operate some machinery, but I would need to have total control over it and know that no-one would interfere. If other people operated the machine without my knowledge, I would potentially be put into a dangerous situation because I would not be able to see what had happened.

I would struggle to get a management level position. Without a degree, I can't cut out part of the career ladder. I would have to start at the bottom, but the bottom is almost impossible for me to get on to. So often the lower-level jobs are the very ones that I can't do. It's not that blind people can't work – my father is blind and works very successfully – but that it is so much harder for us, and society is not well designed to help us.

I am lucky in that my parents are willing and able to look after me. But there is still so much that I can't do, or can only do with expensive aids which I can't afford to buy. At the moment I get mobility and care components of DLA, but even with that many simple tasks are beyond my ability because the aids I could use are too expensive. If the government does not consider this issue then many people will be denied the help they need under the new plans.

One time I was busking on the street and my mum called to ask me to get a melon from the greengrocers. I happily agreed and walked to the grocers, not thinking of how I would find a melon until I got there. I found that I was disorientated by the noise and could not find any way around the store. The only way I could get help was by standing in the narrow doorway until a customer wanted to pass through, and then I had the attention I needed to ask for help. It is funny sometimes what I have to do to get help.

Another time I went into our local petrol station to get some milk. Again my blindness meant I had no way of finding it. I asked the cashiers, but they were thoroughly confused by the situation and did not know what to do or how to help me.

Even shops I know well are impossible for me. The noise and the number of people moving around mean I cannot find my way around the aisles. Even if I could, there is no way I could select the right item. With so much choice I would never know which of many tins is the one I want, or which cardboard box has my cereal, or which milk bottle is the right skimmed level. I would never know if something is on special offer.

If I am buying fresh food, I have no way of telling if what I am selecting is still fresh and good quality. I might walk into a butcher's wanting to buy steak, but the steak available that day didn't look particularly good – I wouldn't know that. I can't tell what is good and what isn't.

As a blind person, I am vulnerable to cheats. Once my dad went to a shop to buy some paint for the garden fence and shed. He was sold a tin that had clearly fallen, cracked and been sealed with masking tape. He didn't know this because he couldn't see it. The tin had lost some of the paint through the crack, so my dad was sold a substandard item because he had no way of knowing. Not everyone is trustworthy.

I never cook for myself. Simple things, like boiling noodles or frozen vegetables, might be okay. But unless I can guess where the hob is by the heat coming off it, I cannot tell where it is to place a saucepan on it. Nor can I judge the heat of a hob or oven. Measuring is impossible and I cannot tell when something is cooked. If there is something spitting in a pan, I cannot tell if it is fine and is just spitting within the pan, or if it is going to spit hot fat onto me.

I can't buy my own clothes. I have no idea what any of the items look like. If I am just staying at home, I don't mind what I wear, but if I am going out then I need a sighted person's opinion. Many times my mum has to tell me things like, "Go and change those trousers," or "If you're going to wear that top, you need to change the jumper." I also can't tell whether or not what I am wearing is clean, unless it smells.

There are so many small things that are hard or even impossible for me to do because I am blind. Because of this my life chances are reduced, and my opportunity for independent living is minimal. My early education showed me how successful I can be if I get the support I need, but this didn't continue. Unless blind people are fully given the support they need, they will be disabled.

11

Gerry's Story: Can You Hear Me?

I've been deaf since birth. My mum caught German measles from my cousin whilst she was pregnant with me. I am profoundly deaf, although I can hear a little bit with the use of hearing aids. The hearing aids are very important to help me communicate, but still my hearing is limited and I have found this depressing at times.

When I was four I was sent to a boarding school for a few years. It was a specialist school for children who were deaf who still had some residual hearing, or who could hear a bit with the use of hearing aids. The school focussed very heavily on lip-reading and talking, and we weren't allowed to sign. To help with this, the teachers had microphones and we all wore headsets and had microphones on our tables.

I was a weekly boarder at my school. Every weekend I went home to my family. School was my home and where I felt I was normal. With my family I felt different, left out because I could not communicate with them as easily as they could communicate amongst themselves. I wanted to be with my family, to feel part of them, but at the same time it was difficult and isolating.

I left education when I was 16. Because I had not been allowed to sign at school, I didn't know any British Sign Language. So when I started attending a Deaf club I wasn't able to communicate easily with all the people there. That was when I started to learn BSL properly, several years after leaving a Deaf school.

After leaving education, I spent a few years working on my parents' farm, and then got a job at a factory. But after nine years the factory closed and I was made redundant. Because I had young children at this time I didn't immediately start looking for work again; I was caring for my children. At this time I also enrolled in some courses.

I wanted to go to college because I wanted to get qualifications to help me get a job. I had no qualifications when I left school; the school focussed so heavily on lip-reading and talking that we were taught very little else. We didn't take any exams. This has meant that, despite my later education, I find written communication difficult; it is because we were not taught a lot of English. So during those years whilst my children were young I attended courses in Maths and English that fitted in with my children's school hours.

Going to college again was difficult. It requires a lot of concentration to keep lip-reading, and following conversation in a group setting can be impossible. After a while my eyes become tired and I develop migraines. Two hours of college in a day was enough to give me a migraine. This exhaustion and pain makes many jobs even harder for me.

When my children were old enough I went to the Jobcentre to sign on for Jobseeker's Allowance, to help me whilst I looked for work. I've been meeting my caseworker every two weeks since signing on. She has been very helpful. She assisted me with applying for ESA and helps me look for jobs. If I find a job I like in a newspaper, I text it to her and she sends off my application for it. She helps me with my applications and keeps my CV up-to-date for me.

It is very difficult for me to find a job. I've had two interviews in this past year but didn't get the jobs. My job options are limited because of my deafness. I can't use a phone at all and I find written communication very difficult, because there are many words which I don't understand. I also only have two qualifications; level 1 in Maths and English.

I am applying for factory work and cleaning work. It has to be something that doesn't involve or rely on a lot of either written or spoken communication, because these are difficult for me. This means that things like reception or admin work are ruled out; my job choices are limited a lot.

Whilst seeking full-time work, with the assistance of my Jobcentre Plus caseworker, I have managed to get work one day a week at a printing company. I'm on a temporary contract, which doesn't give much security, although I have been told that if work picks up I will be offered more hours. Work hasn't picked up – I suppose the recession may have something to do with that. I'm also going to a sewing course twice a week.

At home, my children are very good at alerting me to things like the phone or doorbell. Sometimes they forget, but I have a pager to alert me as well. The pager vibrates in response to the doorbell, phone, burglar alarm and fire alarm, and it has flashing lights that indicate which one. At night, I have a device in my pillow that vibrates in response to the pager, and then I can check the pager to see what it is.

I have a minicom but I don't use it much, as I prefer to text. I don't go out much, because it is tiring and expensive. Dependent on benefits until I can find a job, I don't have much money.

It isn't easy being deaf. Communication is difficult and exhausting and always will be. This isn't ever going to change. I am always going to need assistance with letters and phones. I am always going to get tired and develop migraines from concentrated lip-reading. I am always going to be limited in the jobs I can do. It will always be exhausting to have to be constantly thinking and planning about what I need to do and the help I need to do it.

These things aren't going to change. I'm never going to not need help from society.

I worry about the government's changes. Partly it seems a waste of time and resources – my needs, and the needs of many others, aren't going to change, so why keep assessing what they are? I don't get much support anyway; not enough to compensate the people who I need to help me or pay for the aids and assistance I need.

Being deaf isn't my fault, but it has limited me all my life. It limited my education and limits my career. I am trying as hard as I can, with training courses and mini-jobs and extensive job seeking, but I cannot fully overcome the effects of being deaf. I need the government and society to recognise that I am doing everything I can, but that I need more help to be get the same opportunities that are available to the non-disabled; the opportunities to be educated and to have the physical ability to undertake most jobs.

12

Harriet's Story: Wheelchair Views

One weekend, a year after I developed ME, my parents and I went to stay with my nana and my elder sister. We had a good relaxing time, although my nana and sister were shocked by how easily exhausted I was. We went to church and on a few walks, with me in my wheelchair as usual, and enjoyed watching films together (of course, if I say that, I will be assumed 'fit for work.' Please be aware that when I say 'watch a film' I mean, 'I spent a couple of hours with my family with the TV on. Sitting that long in one place did increase my pain; I did not attempt to concentrate all the way through.'). After the weekend my parents went back home and I stayed on a few more days. During that week, I came across most of the obstacles presented to a wheelchair user in our 'disabled friendly' society.

Going to church, my parents decided to walk as it was a pleasant day. They took me along, pushing my wheelchair. Every slight imperfection in the pavement surface reverberated through the frame of the chair, vibrating up my legs and through my arms. The armrests of the wheelchair were the typical hard black surface, with no padding and no attempt at making a soft or shock absorbing surface. I almost never use the armrests as it hurts too much. This can create a difficult situation, as my hands are often cold and if I rest them on my legs, my body registers the cold as pain. But it is still better than using the armrests.

At this time my parents had not yet bought me a wheelchair with suspension or fitted pneumatic tyres – these reduce pain from vibrations, but are expensive and have the risk of punctures, which wheelchairs with solid tyres do not have. As this was a standard wheelchair, I was quickly uncomfortable from the vibrations. This wasn't even a bad surface! It was recently laid tarmac without cracks, holes or manhole covers; nor were there any branches or stones for my unwitting parents to roll me over. There are much worse places. There are cobbles and uneven flagstones; branches and tree-roots and stones; gravel and manhole covers.

On the way, we had to negotiate some kerbs. This is always interesting. It is common to find that lowered pavements on one side are not reciprocated on the other. Larger kerbs take longer to get up and down, and so, on anything other than a quiet road that serves only the residents, it can be a long time until there is a large enough gap in the traffic to cross from one side to the other. Sometimes, if a strong person is pushing, he (strong enough people are usually male) may half run across the road to take advantage of a smaller gap. Pedestrian crossings are the only place where it can be expected that the pavement and road are level on both sides. These, however, usually have bumped flagstones, which are more painful. Don't get me wrong, I don't wish these flag stones to be removed (I know they are useful for those who are blind), but it is not something that would occur to most people as being a difficulty for wheelchair users.

Kerbs are a good test of the strength and ability of your handler (yes, handler is the term used for those who push wheelchairs. It makes me feel like a dog, or recalcitrant pony!). Going down a kerb, a strong handler is required to let the wheelchair gently down, rolling off the edge of the kerb using the back wheels only. Not everyone is strong enough and there can be some nasty bumps down onto the road. Some people just roll straight off, coming close to tipping me out on several occasions. I save myself by gripping the armrests. Advice on going down kerbs (for care workers – my wheelchair manual says to go forward) is to take the wheelchair and its user down backwards, but I dislike being pulled around as though I am nothing more than a wheeled suitcase. I may be chronically ill, but I would like to be treated as a fellow human. I don't always have the choice though, as kerbs are not built with wheelchair users in mind.

Once safely across the road, the wheelchair needs to be tilted again to go up the kerb. Anything over 1cm requires the wheelchair to be tipped back, lifting the front castors off the ground until they are level with the pavement. Then the wheelchair is rolled forward and, if necessary, lifted to get the back wheels on as well. My brother is excellent at this and can manage large kerbs with great smoothness and comfort for me – he is strong and considerate, and has had a lot of practice. Other people are less good, and may need several attempts, or land with another bump. It isn't easy, even with a handler and in the few places where the pavement is lowered. Getting the wheelchair positioned correctly takes time, which is not always available when cars are using the road as well. Another option is to be taken up backwards; again this adds to the length of time spent in the road with the more usual road users.

Novice wheelchair handlers are always surprised at how small a bump, such as a kerb or door-rim, is sufficient to stop the wheelchair. I have been almost thrown out several times by someone who expected the wheelchair to roll over the impediment, and then found that it wouldn't. It is common to find entrances to shops or other public buildings have slight door rims that are too big to roll over, and this makes them inaccessible for anyone in a self-propelled wheelchair. It doesn't matter how strong you are; the physics of small front wheels means that the castors will not roll over anything over 2cm in height. If it is not too big then backwards is an option, but again there is the risk of yourself or your belongings falling out, and too big a step cannot be taken backwards either.

The other big difficulty with pavements is that they all slope towards the road. These pavements were no exception. It makes pushing very difficult, because one hand has to pull back on the handle furthest from the road to prevent the wheelchair from turning into it. Self-propelling at times becomes impossible, because so much effort has to be put into braking one side of the wheelchair.

Sometimes I wistfully think how good it would be to have a wheelchair-driving course. Something to teach the handler how to negotiate the outside with maximum comfort for the person in the wheelchair. Learning to avoid rolling over sticks and stones (which don't break, but definitely hurt, my bones) would be a good start! And being able to get up and down kerbs, remember how far my feet are in front of the wheelchair, have the strength to push me up slopes and be able to hold the chair when going down would be useful.

A couple of days after this trip to church, I was taken to Hobbycraft by my sister. The wonderful thing about shops is that they have much smoother surfaces, sometimes even with carpet tiles, which are (relative) bliss to roll on. We mooched around the store, admiring the range of crafts available. There was one that was new to us – Sketch by Numbers. Painting by Numbers was something I loved as a child, and I have recently completed one my sister bought for me. That kind of thing is about right for me – a little painful on the finger joints, a little messy as my hands shake a bit from tiredness, but requiring just the right amount of mental effort that doesn't exhaust me but also occupies my entire mind, so I am not left with worrying thoughts harrying my mind.

I admired things on my eye level. I can't stoop to anything close to the ground, or reach anything more than five feet above me. On a previous trip to try on some new walking shoes (not for long distance walking, you understand. Just something to support my feet as I get around the house) I couldn't reach up to put a pair back, or get a different size down. It makes shopping alone, even if I had the strength to self-propel and could negotiate all the pavements and shop entrances, an impossibility. I'm not sure what I would do about groceries either, as I cannot see myself wheeling around a shop, collecting items, and putting them into a trolley. Internet shopping is a possibility, but delivery charges are high, particularly for small purchases, and quality cannot be checked before payment.

My sister placed the items she wanted on my lap. 'Is that alright?' she asked. 'Of course,' I replied. 'I'm glad to be of some use to you!'

I meant it. Being in a wheelchair, I am aware how much effort I necessarily demand from my family and friends. I like to help out where I can. It isn't always possible though. I sometimes go grocery shopping with my mum, just to get a few extra things, and then I cannot take the shopping on my lap. The weight of it is painful. My friends and family aren't shy of telling me how much of an effort it is to push a wheelchair. Hot days, slopes, cambered pavements, kerbs – they all add to the difficulty and make what could be a pleasant walk for them into a chore.

The next day we went on a visit to a zoo. We were all excited. Despite my conservation background, that carefully noses out just how many of the animals kept there are listed as 'not currently threatened', I still love zoos. My favourites are the monkeys (black and white colobus monkeys at this zoo) and the lemurs. Their long limbs and tails give them an adorable floppy look; I can imagine one wrapping its arms around my neck and giving me a hug. Their agility makes them a delight to watch, as they leap off posts to catch hanging ropes or swing from one bar to another. I don't feel too bad for them either, as they appear to have enough space and opportunity to be happy practicing their gymnastics.

At the entrance to the zoo, my sister went down to reception to ask to borrow a wheelchair whilst Nana and I waited in the car. Once she came back, I got in and Nana went off to park. It was a steep slope down to reception, so I applied the brakes to make it easier for my sister to prevent the wheelchair from getting away. Unfortunately, the pneumatic tyres were a little flat, so the brakes weren't quite as effective as could be desired! Wheelchair brakes are not meant to be used to slow or stop a wheelchair, but only to keep it parked. The brakes press onto the tyre, so using them to slow the wheelchair means wearing down the tyre. When self-propelling, it is difficult to control the wheelchair going downhill. Even with a handler I often have to apply the brakes (it is too much effort for me to use my hands on the handrims to slow the chair, and the friction can be painful) to prevent the wheelchair from going too fast.

The zoo was spread over undulating ground, and my sister had to stop several times for a rest. Very few people can cope with pushing me on sloped ground for very long.

We stopped to look at the flamingos with their mirrors (used to relax them into feeling part of a larger flock), and then the rhinos grazing placidly further up the hill. We missed out the cheetah (or perhaps it was a leopard. I couldn't get near enough to tell) as it was positioned on a slope too steep for my sister.

Later on, we used the road-train to give my sister a rest. Pushing wheelchairs is not easy. The road train was full, but there is a carriage with a ramp that prioritises wheelchair users. Some people had to get off for us; I hoped they found a seat further back. I know healthy people often complain about making way for wheelchair users and the disabled. I have upset people on trains before by asking that they move so that I can use the dedicated wheelchair space. I say I upset someone; this is just what the station staff told me when he had got the ramp positioned and asked the lady to move for me, before he took me onto the train. Why can't we just get on with it, the way they do? The fact is, we are already 'getting on with it' *way* more than they do. In this particular case, we were using the road train for my sister's benefit, not mine. She was tired. If you had been pushing an adult around in a wheelchair, you would be tired too.

At the end of the day, we tried to return to the car. My sister struggled to push me up the hill. Half way up, I said I would get out and walk. I could at that time manage about 50m a day in one go, and reckoned that was how far away the car was. I figured that by the time I had shuffled that far, I would be as tired as my sister was from pushing me around all day. Besides, I could see that the car park was gravelled, and there is no way I ever want the pain and discomfort of being pushed over that. It isn't easy for the handler either. My sister appreciated my offer, and took the wheelchair back to reception. I sat on a bench and waited for her to come back, and then leant on her arm to help take a bit of my weight off my legs.

Getting back to my parents involved using the train. I can only use a train if I book at least 24 hours in advance, to ensure that the wheelchair space is reserved for me and that station staff will bring ramps to get me on and off the trains. This journey, unusually, had no hitches. Most often the station staff are unaware that I am coming even though I have booked assistance. This is generally okay for getting onto a train if there is someone with me to find a member of station staff and tell them I need assistance. Getting off is more worrying. Usually the guard on the train will ring ahead and come to check that I can get off the train before it leaves, but that does not always happen. I frequently have to ask members of public to find someone to bring a ramp for me. Dame Tanni Grey-Thompson has had to crawl off a train because no-one came to help her.

Public transport in general can be an interesting experience. Transport for London introduced ramps at 16 of its tube stations during the Olympics, but my experience of being left on trains combined with the number of people using the Tube and short waits at stations meant I certainly didn't plan to try using the Tube. Even if I did, I would be severely restricted by the lack of lifts and TfL's refusal to put any money towards improving disabled access. Buses aren't much better. One man has reported 28 refusals for access to a bus in 18 months.

The government wants to class anyone who can propel themselves 200m as mobile, but they haven't stopped to think how many places are inaccessible because of slopes, steps or kerbs and door rims. Ever tried propelling yourself up a hill? Did you notice that gravity pulls you back down? Ever tried to get around a busy shop with narrow aisles, or open a door you cannot reach at the same time as propel yourself through it? There are a myriad of obstacles that a healthy person doesn't even notice, and very few destinations within 200m of each other. I am genuinely scared that the people making these decisions don't have the knowledge, experience or basic consideration for others' circumstances to make the right decision.

Back at home, I went on Facebook. I am a member of a couple of ME/CFS support groups and like to read what is going on. Comments of support, shared experiences, fear about applying for DLA or ESA, appeals and tribunals, success or struggles with GPs and Physios. It all helps to make me feel a little less alone. That day, someone had posted a link to a new group. I forget its name, but the person posting the link was recommending that we report the group to Facebook, as a hate group. I clicked on the link.

The group claimed it isn't a hate group. It is a 'group to revoke handicapped parking permits', and claims to be more of a joke than a hate group. I don't believe it.

Stop treating people differently based on their physical capabilities, that's what they say, but it's all lip service! As soon as one of those handicapped people wants to park a car they don't want to be treated 'like everybody else' anymore. Well, here at the group to revoke handicapped parking permits we say: "May every man, woman, child, and retard, be treated equally."

Do they really need it? If they're so messed up they can't drive, then why doesn't the person they're with just drop them off and find a fucking spot? If they are able to drive, but use a wheelchair then there's absolutely no need for a close spot- they're on wheels, a conveyance that's gonna get them there easily and faster anyway. Now for those who are just so weak and tired that they aren't able to drive and have too much pride to get in a wheelchair- I say stay home! You've probably got somebody catering to your every need there, too! Why do you feel you need to get that kind of attention when you leave the house as well?

Last week I was reminded of how EQUAL parking availability is in Paris. Despite my sister's limping and pain she doesn't expect bullshit for parking or special preference in the metro. Dog, I love Paris, they don't ruin architecture for the disabled either.

I wish people would understand. I used to say I wouldn't wish ME on anyone, even to make them understand, it's that bad. With the rhetoric from the media and government, I'm more inclined now to wish the people making the decisions and writing the papers could have it, at least for a few years, so that they can understand what they are doing. No, I can't drive more than a few miles, and not at all on many days. It requires concentration and reaction speeds that are beyond me when I am tired, which I would be if I drove further. I could manage more, but being a generally sensible person I am not going to go anywhere near my limit of driving. Yes,

I use a wheelchair. I'm not bothered about what people think of me for using it. It's only ignorant people who would think badly of me. No, it isn't quicker or easier to use a wheelchair. For a start, it means I need someone with me who is strong enough to push me. Then, the wheelchair has to be got out of the car, which requires space at the back to get it out without being in the way of passing cars, and space at the side to get it round to me. Other people have more medical equipment, which needs more space than I do. I can just about cope with a normal parking space, provided other cars are parked straight. Which doesn't always happen. Once the wheelchair is out, travel in it is slower than an average person walking. Of course it is, the handler is pushing a heavy weight. It also isn't easier. Alright, it's easier for me to be in a wheelchair than to walk, but sitting in a wheelchair, going over rough ground (anything that isn't a carpet or large smooth tiles without visible joins) is harder for me than walking is for you, a healthy person. And walking is so hard for me, that my arthritic nana sometimes pushes my wheelchair a little way, because it is less tiring and painful for her to push me than it is for me to walk, even without pushing a wheelchair. When I do walk, I get overtaken by pensioners with their walking sticks and Zimmer frames.

As for people catering for my every need; well, not quite. There are some things I am fortunate enough to be able to do. I wash and dress myself, albeit very slowly. And I can just about manage to get my own breakfast and lunch, as long as I rest afterwards. Yes, my parents wash my clothes, prepare my cooked meals, clean the house, take me to doctor's appointments and the pharmacist. But I don't have people 'catering to my every need' out of choice. It is out of necessity. And I refuse to consider that it is acceptable to leave me poorly fed, lonely, and house bound for no better reason than that I have been so unlucky as to develop a debilitating chronic illness.

Sure, there are 'perks' to being disabled. Like having the council help you access public places by providing you with the space you need. But then, there are a lot of perks from being healthy too. You can walk. You can run, you can dance, you can leap for joy or curl up in sorrow. You can cook a meal or go out to a restaurant on a whim. You can play sport or do some knitting, bake a cake or play catch with your nieces and nephews. You can stay up late chatting with friends, go out clubbing, or get up early to watch the sun rise and listen to the dawn chorus. You can hold down a job, raise a family and meet friends at the weekends. You can wind down with a glass of wine, or wake yourself up with a cup of coffee.

You can go where you want, when you want, and aren't prohibited from places by their not having large enough parking spaces. You are not blocked from accessing a shop because it has a slight raise across the doorway, or because your handler is too tired or weak to get you up a slope. You can access all Grade I or II listed buildings that are open to the public. You can go up and down steps and ladders, and can cross narrow foot bridges and climb over stiles. You can walk up hills, follow rivers, climb rock faces. You can get any bus, or catch a train without having to give twenty-four hours' notice to the train stations at which you wish to get on, off or change trains. You are not dependent on the availability of a strong and willing person to get out of your house.

I can't do any of those things. I can't walk, certainly will not be running, dancing or jumping any time soon, and as for curling up – my joints hurt enough without putting them under such stress. I don't have the strength to cook a meal or sufficient freedom from pain to be able to wield a knife. Anything after 10pm is late and anything before 8am is early – and I rest during the day as well. I can do less in one week than you can achieve in your evenings and weekends on top of work and maintaining a household. Alcohol and caffeine I avoid as if they were poisons – indeed alcohol in combination with my medications would be lethal. I can't get myself around, so am dependant on people coming to me and being willing to help me. I love historic buildings, but anything Grade 1 or 2 listed does not have to provide disabled access. I don't mind this, but I do mind shops and other public buildings that do not have automatic doors, have steps or large doorway trims, or have aisles too narrow for wheelchairs to access. Buses I haven't even tried, and trains I have to ring in advance to ask for assistance getting on and off. Pavements are a penance – to pay for my crime of needing a wheelchair, perhaps.

So next time you complain of the 'perks' available to the disabled and chronically ill, remember this: however many adjustments are made to help us, we never have as many perks as you.

13

Ian's Story: The Cost of Care

My sister was born three months prematurely in February 1980 and was not given a diagnosis of Asperger Syndrome/ learning difficulties until she was around the age of 14 (sometime during 1996). This was partly due to the limited awareness about Asperger Syndrome during the time my sister was a child. Asperger Syndrome, named after the Austrian paediatrician Hans Asperger (1906 – 1980) is a fairly new discovery and was not a standard diagnosis until 1992, when it was included in the World Health Organisations diagnostic manual, The International Classification of Diseases.

Despite these limitations, my parents were very aware that there was something rather different about my sister. When she was a toddler, she would avoid any interaction with her fellow toddlers at mother/baby groups and stay within close proximity of her parents at all times. She didn't speak until she was almost three and communicated her feelings by singing. When she did talk for the first time, it was a full sentence observing the changing colours of a leaf in autumn rather than the usual one or two words that a child would utter for the first time.

She had a rather difficult time through school as she got older. In primary school, the differences between her and her friends were minimal and she managed to maintain friendships with several girls from her class – often having them stay with us after school. As she got older, however, her difficulties became more apparent and she became a constant victim of bullying because her fellow pupils saw her as 'weird'. During secondary school, all her friends had completely deserted her and she found herself alone, isolated, confused and victimised.

Throughout this period, my parents (knowing there was something about her) were trying to find support from social services and several evening sessions for people struggling with school were provided for her. Despite my parents' best efforts, the bullying she was receiving at school in addition to family problems at the time led to her suffering a mental breakdown when she was fifteen. She was sectioned under the mental health act and stayed in an adolescent's mental health unit for a lot of that year. During this time, she went through periods of hyper-mania, extreme depression, hallucinations and confusion.

She never fully recovered and has been on medication for depression ever since but returned back to school on a part time basis a year later and sat English, Maths and Art GCSE exams – passing Art with a grade B. It was around this time that she was diagnosed with Asperger Syndrome and she started to attend a school for autistic children. She also attended various colleges and youth groups that catered for her needs (or at least to the best of their ability).

My sister is a well-meaning and good natured individual who needs (and craves for) social interaction and to be occupied with meaningful activities during the evenings as well as during the daytime. Sadly, this is rarely provided in the residential care homes in which she has lived since reaching adulthood. My sister has always known that she is not as socially aware as other people her age. She finds it very upsetting that she is not able to seek a career, live by herself or, most importantly, make friends. The frustration, coupled with her limited ability to understand and deal with emotions, has led to her displaying some very complex behaviour over the years. Over time, her behaviour has deteriorated and she has almost become 'more autistic.'

She has been in various residential care homes since reaching adulthood and has been at her current address for several years now. A problem for her at the moment is that she is incredibly bored at the home she's living in. Residents are well looked after in terms of being well fed, clean and so on, but there is a lot of 'dead time', where nothing much is going on. Residents have to occupy themselves. This is especially the case during the evenings.

For some, this isn't a problem as a television or games console will provide enough entertainment for most evenings. My sister, however, retreats to her own room for hours and will drive herself to distraction with reoccurring negative thoughts about her situation. I have seen how this lack of social and meaningful interaction has impacted on her. She has retreated into herself just as she has retreated into her room, because those caring for her do not go beyond physical care. This would be greatly lessened if she had things to do and people who take an interest in her. Instead, her residential care staff are often not paid well enough to be willing to go beyond their call of duty. It is rare, almost non-existent, that any of her carers take any interest in her and her needs. A higher salary might attract people who want to provide more meaningful care and who are more interested in engaging with service users, even where such engagement is costly in time and effort.

The council are paying for my sister to be in care (amongst many others) and have only recently been questioning where a lot of the money is being spent. I am confident to say that a part of her difficulties at the moment have been due to inadequate support from the authorities in charge of her care. In my experience of working for the National Autistic Society, a large proportion of day centres and care homes are managed with profit making as a higher priority than providing for the needs of the service users (a lot of whom are unable to speak out about their needs). I have worked at a college for autistic adults that was very swiftly transformed into a day centre. Many of the teaching staff were made redundant and invited to reapply for their jobs but with a 30% salary cut. This led to a whole work team of new staff who (although having the best intentions) were nowhere near as qualified or even interested as the previous staff members. Lessons soon became holding activities and many service users started to regress rather than improve. The area manager who had made this decision had previously been the manager of a dog food factory and was hired for his financial abilities rather than any empathy with autism. The few times I met him, I found him to be patronising and apathetic towards the service users I was working with, and cared greatly for. It is a tragedy that money is allowed to be put above people's needs.

In conclusion, a lot of care providers are being run with finance being the most important factor. Without denying its importance, the quality of life for service users is of paramount importance and should be the first priority in provision of care.

14

James' Story: Surviving the Benefits System

I've been on Incapacity Benefit since 2005. I guess that makes me one of the people 'abandoned' to 'fester'. It's not really like that. I've been on benefits that long because I've been ill that long; or longer if you take into account the time for which I was ill before I went on IB.

I have a degree in Fine Art, but even long before the recession and before so many people went to university it wasn't exactly a degree with great career prospects. Consequently after university I was on Jobseeker's briefly whilst I looked for jobs. Even then it wasn't easy being on benefits; there were conditions and sanctions that weren't always compatible with what was best for the person. I started a training course but left after the trial period, as a mutual decision between me and the employer. Despite this mutual agreement on what was best, I was given a six-month sanction and my benefits were reduced by more than 50%.

It was a horrible time. I knew I was right and should not have been sanctioned, and so I had appealed the decision, but in the meantime I was getting very little money. I was very poor in depressing circumstances, and it was difficult to survive. I was in a bedsit to save as much money as I could but I couldn't stop the start of depression and mental illness as I struggled to live. For six months this continued; poverty and depression while I waited for the appeal to rectify the government's mistake. In the meantime I was the one who had to pay for it, despite it not being my mistake.

I won the appeal. My money was back-paid but it didn't change the fact that for six months I had been in poverty and depressed. Nothing could change those six months and future money is no use at the moment when you need to buy food or electricity or heating.

Once the appeal was sorted and I no longer had all the stress and stuff to deal with I went back into education. From there I continued in work for the next couple of decades. For a while I ran an off-licence for a relative, and then I became a retail manager. So I was doing well for myself and was a competent worker: 'doing the right thing,' in government parlance.

But then I had a nervous breakdown. Every month I had to get sick-notes from my doctor to send to what was then the Department of Social Security, now the Department of Work and Pensions. Finally after six months I was signed off long-term, on the basis of a questionnaire and doctor's report. It was a massive relief as at last I had a secure source of income. Secure income is very important for mental health, as successive government reports have noted. It makes sense. If you're worried or scared about income, in or close to poverty and struggling to look after yourself adequately then it's almost inevitable that you will experience anxiety and depression related problems.

My benefits have been reassessed every year. My first reassessment included a medical assessment, which was then the Personal Capability Assessment. It's not as harsh as the Work Capability Assessment but still one of the toughest in the world. I was very nervous and it was difficult and upsetting, but I decided I have nothing to be ashamed of and just had to tell the truth – all of it, however difficult. I was very fortunate. The person assessing me had experienced similar issues many years ago so he knew very well what I was going through and the difficulties with work that it presented.

My second assessment a year later was in a different building. It was a cold and depressing place. I was kept waiting at the reception desk to register my attendance whilst the receptionists stood a small distance away and chatted. The assessment was okay; I didn't feel there was any understanding from my assessor but my benefits were continued so there must have been a bit of comprehension, or maybe I explained well enough.

The next time around was much worse. The person assessing me was curt and abrasive. There was no sign of concern, interest or understanding about me, my condition or the problems I faced. I was very uncomfortable right from the start and rapidly felt panicky. By the end I was miserable, humiliated and exhausted. It was a horrible experience, deeply distressing and in no way helpful for my health.

All this time I was struggling greatly. I don't have a landline or internet, so it has been very difficult to stay aware of everything that is going on or to contact the DWP. For a long time I had no social interaction at all. I found my way to a great church and they have helped me a lot with opportunities to make friends and do a bit of volunteering when I am able. They also allow me to use their phone and internet, which is a massive help. I'm very worried about the government's plans to do almost all benefits management online. How am I supposed to deal with all the things the DWP wants me to do when I don't have internet, and getting out of my house isn't always easy for me?

More recently, I was transferred from IB to ESA. I was put in the Work-Related Activity Group, meaning that at some (unknown) point I may be able to return to work. Because at some point I might be able to work, I am expected to remain 'close to the job market,' by whatever means the DWP deems necessary.

My first meeting with my Jobcentre advisor went well. I felt okay with what was happening. My advisor was sympathetic and not at all rude. However the appointment was only 40 minutes long. With seven years of health history to go through, there was far from a sufficient amount of time to give an adequate history. With complex medical needs there was no possibility for 40 minutes to ever be enough time.

It was arranged that I would go back in a month's time. I did so. To my distress, this meeting was held in a public room. Sitting next to me was another person discussing their needs with their advisor. There were multiple people in the room and all of them could hear what I said, just as I could hear what they said. Apart from being a distraction it was inappropriate for such confidential information to be discussed in a public place. We were talking about personal and upsetting things that I did not wish to make available to other people. But I felt I had to play by their rules.

The advisor was a little less sympathetic this time. Perhaps she thought that one month was enough time for a seven-year illness to start improving. She was firing things at me constantly: I should get involved in charity work, I should get active, I could do this, I ought to try that. Here's a good one for you, you like the outdoors don't you? You could cycle around looking for fly-tipping and tell the fire service (seriously, if that's a public service, why isn't it paid?).

I tried to tell her that I already was involved in charity work at my church, on my own initiative getting used to a work pattern again. This work was great for me because it was supported, interesting and allowed me to start using my art degree again. But she didn't listen and wasn't interested in what I was doing; she seemed to just want to tick boxes and get me doing what the DWP said I should do, not what was good for me. Church volunteering didn't fit what they wanted, or it wasn't something they had told me to do, so it didn't count.

I had been feeling the pressure of having to go every four weeks. It's a very difficult thing to do when you're poor and ill. My health had started to deteriorate because of it, so we agreed that I wouldn't go in again for another two to three months.

At the end of this time I went back to meet my adviser. Immediately she asked, "Have you looked into any of this?" I was fully honest. I hadn't looked into it. I had been having a bad time with my illness and was struggling enough to keep on with my current volunteering when I was more ill. Finding time, energy and health to look into *extra* volunteering on top of what I was doing had not been possible. At once my adviser became stern and pushy. She was cross that I hadn't looked into the volunteering she had told me to investigate, and didn't care that I was already doing work, off my own initiative, and that my health simply didn't cooperate with anyone's timetables or plans. Health doesn't work like that.

Soon after this I was sent a medical questionnaire for my next assessment for incapacity benefits (now ESA). I wasn't doing at all well with my health and didn't manage to send the form in on time. Instead of being sent a reminder, I was given an appointment to see a health care professional for the Work Capability Assessment. I never filled in the questionnaire.

At the assessment, the assessor was friendly and tried to put me at my ease. He told me about the changes between IB and ESA, to let me know what to expect. The assessment focussed on my specific problems, rather than asking questions that have no relation to me. I answered as truthfully and as cooperatively as I could. At the end, he said, "I think you can work with the right support and a bit of time."

I was surprised by that. He had been very understanding all the way through and seemed to believe what I was saying. Certainly nothing I knew of my health over the last seven years indicated that I would recover with just a 'bit' of time! But when the decision came through I had been put in the Support Group, so maybe what he meant by 'the right support and a bit of time' was different from what I thought he meant at the time.

It is a huge relief to be put back in the Support Group. But it shouldn't be this huge. There shouldn't be a feeling of relief that it's 'not me, not this time.' Sick people should have confidence that they will be met with fair treatment and justice, but they're not getting it. I've been lucky to largely get the finances I need, but I shouldn't feel that it is luck.

The 'help' I received from the Jobcentre was no use. There was no intention of considering my specific case. There was no recognition that I already have got regular volunteering. Even worse, there was no recognition of what type of volunteering I can do. Some of my inability to work is due to mental illnesses, but there was no understanding of mental health. There was no comprehension of the reality of what happens when a brain breaks. It was as if conditions like Alzheimer's or epilepsy, or the effects of things like a stroke or a lesion of the brain, had nothing useful to say on the effects of mental illnesses.

Help needs to be individualised and multidisciplinary. It also needs to be from highly skilled people. Advisers need detailed knowledge of both their clients' health conditions and its impacts, and of the job market and opportunities available for people with these limitations. It would be great to have people from the employment and voluntary sectors to set out in more detail what help they can offer, what skills are needed and what training is useful. Unless employers help out, the whole exercise becomes useless, as I won't have the skills that anyone wants. It's just ticking DWP boxes, without improving employability.

I need work that engages my brain. It's not that I'm dismissive of unskilled labour; I've done my time in fast food chains. But as government reports have recognised, work that is monotonous or repetitive with little or no autonomy is bad for mental health.[137] So as someone who already has mental health issues, this type of work simply isn't appropriate. It will make my health deteriorate with the consequence that I spend even longer out of work.

I have received counselling in the past, but the funding was withdrawn from my local GP surgery. I can't access large towns and cities because of my health conditions, so have had to continue without counselling. It's all part of chronic underinvestment in genuine effective support.

I certainly hope to get back into work, and I'm taking my own steps towards it. Like most people on ESA, I'm not work-shy. I'd love to work. But the DWP and the Jobcentre are not helping. With little security in finances, no social networks, distinct lack of confidence of fair treatment, imbalance between effort and reward, and

[137] Dame Carol Black, 2007, Working for a healthier tomorrow, DWP

frequent lack of autonomy or control, the entire system seems to have been set up in such a way that it actively causes deterioration in claimant's health.[138]

[138] Ibid. These are some of the provisos identified as hindering the otherwise positive relationship between work and health.

15

Epilogue

These stories have shown how unpredictable health is. It isn't possible to guarantee that your child or grandchild will not be born with an incurable illness or permanent disability. Nor is it possible to guarantee that you yourself will never be chronically sick or disabled. Illnesses like ME and Guillan-Barre can come at any time without warning. Other illnesses might cause a steady decline into loss of work ability, even as the sufferer tries to keep working. Sometimes the striving to keep on, the insistence on not being weak and not giving in, can be the very thing that causes, exacerbates or prolongs the crash into chronic ill-health. Sometimes there is nothing we could have done differently or better to prevent it from coming, or to make it go away.

Sometimes our bodies break down. That's just how life is. It can happen to anyone.

We can't insure against this type of thing. It is too inefficient and expensive for every individual to have private health insurance. But what we can have, and should have, is a society where everyone recognises that it could have been them today, and it might yet be them tomorrow.

What do we need for a system that works for the chronically ill and disabled? We need one that accurately assesses people's health, needs and abilities. We need benefits that adequately cover subsistence needs and extra health costs. We need specialised personal caseworkers, who will work with the chronically ill and disabled to determine what work actually exists that they can do. We need a recognition of the difference between permanent, unchanging disability and chronic illness. We need assistance into employment and assistance for the employers to help them employ chronically ill and disabled people.

In 2003, the OECD concluded that, "No single country ... can be said to have a particularly successful policy for disabled people."[139] The following suggestions are based partly on this report. They are written to be suggestions of possible directions that social policy could be taken in, in order to improve the wellbeing and employment of disabled and chronically ill people in this country.

Inaccurate assessment

Many problems with the current system appear to be related to inaccurate assessments. This may be because of inaccuracies in reporting, inappropriate inferences made from what a claimant says, lack of understanding of a given condition, or poor quality of decision making. The high rate of appeals suggests that claimants do not feel they are having an adequate assessment of their health and abilities, and the high success rate of appeals suggests that many claimants are being incorrectly told that they are fit for work. It is vital for a working social system that assessments are accurate.

Accurate assessment requires the compilation of detailed information regarding the claimant's state of health. This can come from the medical notes of the claimant, as well as other evidence submitted by all medical care professionals who are involved in the care and treatment of the claimant. Wherever possible this should include submissions from specialists in the claimant's condition(s). There may also be an assigned caseworker who is responsible for ensuring that all evidence is collated.

Assessments may be better conducted if split into two parts, as suggested by the OECD. These would be a medical assessment of functional ability, with a wide range of specialists available for less familiar or more complex cases, and an assessment of work capacity, carried out by

---

[139] OECD 2003, Transforming Disability into Ability. All quotes in this chapter, unless specified otherwise, are from this source

vocational specialists. Disability assessments should be based on the social, not medical, model of disability.

Disability status as recognised by this procedure should not be affected by any attempts at work-related measures, such as trying work for a short period of time. Disability status should only be changed after a medical assessment demonstrates a change in the disability.

Re-testing is unnecessary for permanent disabilities. The aim of re-testing should be "not so much to withdraw benefit payments as to identify people who should (again) be offered rehabilitation or re-employment services."

Inadequate benefits

There are many costs associated with disability. To make society more equitable, and to ensure decent living standards for everyone, these costs should be met by society. DLA-type payments, in the UK and a few other countries, have been criticised by the OECD for compensating "only very high costs" and hence being "only accessible for a small group of severely disabled people." The government should therefore consider an extension of DLA to give better coverage.

Benefits given for health reasons should give an adequate income and be a secure income source. Currently, claimants risk losing their disabled status by attempting work. There should be provision for claimants to try to work without losing their disabled status or having to re-apply for benefit if their attempt at work proves unsuccessful. In Belgium, claimants can try work for up to 14 days; this is advantageous for employers, who don't have to go through a new cycle of guaranteed wage payment, and for employees, as these days count as part of the waiting period for a disability application.

A few countries offer, or have offered in the past, partial benefits. This means that those who can manage part-time work only can also receive benefit to ensure an adequate income. It means that those who cannot work full-time for health reasons, but who can do some work, are assisted to do so without losing all benefit entitlement.

Some countries have special rehabilitation benefits; this has the advantage of special eligibility conditions, wider population coverage and disconnection from other benefits.

The need for individual caseworkers

Disabled and chronically ill people face a variety of challenges in obtaining feasible work. These vary hugely from person to person, depending not only on the individual's condition and its severity, but also on the combination of conditions, work experience, qualifications, and support available for home life. This means that the support an individual needs and the possibilities for particular types of work vary hugely. To give effective support, that support needs to be tailored to the individual. This is likely to require a dedicated, individual and personal case worker who has knowledge of both the individual's condition(s) and the limitations these create, and also knowledge of the jobs, programmes and support that are available and suitable. "Caseworkers will need an extensive knowledge of the range of available benefits and services. More time will be required to assist individuals and follow each case."

Iceland has a programme in which individuals are requested to report on their work experience, qualifications and hobbies as well as their state of health.[140] The individual is also asked to say what he or she thinks would need to occur to make work possible. This means that there is recognition that individuals with the same health condition may have different work capabilities, e.g. because of differences in qualifications and experience. The caseworker then works with the individual to explore what employment exists, if any, that the individual may be capable of undertaking.

Intervention should occur early on. Early intervention is associated with higher returns to employment. According to the OECD, "average per capita costs for

[140] Konráðsdóttir 2011, Work ability assessment - description and evaluation of a new tool in vocational rehabilitation and in disability claims, Master's thesis

vocational rehabilitation and training is low compared to the average cost of a disability benefit. Provided that such intervention secures permanent employment, investment should pay off within a short period." In several countries, applications for incapacity benefits are treated as applications for vocational rehabilitation. Currently, there is no support given during Statutory Sick Pay (28 weeks) or during the assessment phase for ESA (can be over 13 weeks), meaning that more than 9 months can pass before any support is given. This may be wasted time, in which exploration of different work possibilities could have occurred.

Intervention should recognise that there will be individuals who are not able to undertake any work. Intervention should also include activities "that are not strictly considered as work but contribute to the social integration of the disabled person."

Understanding the variations in disability

Disabled and chronically ill people form a heterogeneous group. Individuals may be disabled or chronically ill from birth, or their impairment may come later after a gradual or sudden onset. They may be able to continue to work in the same job, or unable to continue in the same job but able to work in something else, or be unable to continue to work at present, or they may expect never to be able to work. The illness or disability may remain static, or it may degenerate, fluctuate, be expected to improve, or have no predictability about prognosis and future ability to work.

A successful social programme needs to recognise all of this. It needs to recognise that some people may have skills that are not wholly impaired by their illness or disability, whilst others with a different skill subset but the same illness or disability may lose all of their ability. It needs to recognise that some people will always have the same needs and can work as long as those needs are fully met. It needs to recognise that some people may need time to adjust, time to stabilise or time to rehabilitate before they can work. It needs to recognise that some people may be able to do some work now, but that long-term health and work ability would be higher if the person were allowed to make a full, sustained recovery first. It needs to recognise that some people may vary on a monthly, weekly, daily, or even hourly basis in the type, quality and quantity of work they can do.

It also needs to recognise that some people just cannot work, because their health or disability does not permit it, or because the personal cost would be disproportionate.

Assisted employment

The OECD said that, "Involving employers is crucial to the successful integration of disabled persons." This may be through means ranging from "moral suasion and anti-discrimination legislation to mandatory employment quotas." The success of these measures depends largely on the enforcement of non-compliance penalties.

"Apart from legal loopholes, another reason for ineffectiveness appears to be that employers need help to fulfil their obligations." Therefore programmes need to be in place that help employers to employ people with disabilities or long-term illness. This includes matters like the Access to Work programme, which pays for practical support to assist with work, and supported employment.

Programmes to help disabled and chronically ill people include subsidised, sheltered and supported employment. Supported employment is personal assistance given on-the-job or in training to the employer or employee. Sheltered employment is employment that is in a segregated environment; this can be in a special workshop, social firm or protected job in the open labour market. Subsidised employment is when the employer is compensated for part of the labour costs of a disabled employee. Disabled and chronically ill people may also need work that is flexible in hours worked on a range of timescales, with allowances made for changes in work ability if health is not consistent.

Disability programmes must include the awareness that not all disabled or chronically ill people can work. Programmes should operate to discourage exclusion from the labour market and to prevent social isolation; if work is not possible then there should be encouragement and assistance to enable other forms of participation in society.

Disability programmes cannot be expected to solve problems in the labour market. If the problem is with demand, then this needs to be addressed.

Appendix 1: Government Spending

In 2010/11, the government spent £696 billion and collected £548 billion in tax receipts.[141] The population at that time was around 62 million.[142] This means that the government spent an average £11,225 per person. As revenue is raised from a variety of sources, I am using Income Tax as a proxy for all forms of tax and other revenue. This means that I am assuming that tax such as National Insurance, VAT, alcohol and tobacco duties, road tax etc. are paid in proportion to Income Tax. Income tax forms 27% of tax receipts. Tax receipts do not cover government expenditure, but in an ideal world they would, so I shall calculate the figures as if 27% of government expenditure was sourced from Income Tax (Income Tax as a percentage of government expenditure in fact forms 21.5%).

If a person lives for 80 years, then the government spends £8.98 million on that person on average. If 27% of this expenditure was sourced from Income Tax, then over a working life, a person needs to earn enough to pay £245,820 in Income Tax. Assuming a 50 year working life (18 to 68), this is £4,916 each year. In 2010/11, the personal tax allowance was £6,475 and income between £6,475 and £43,875 was taxed at 20%. However the tax boundaries have changed, so to assess current requirements it is more accurate to use 2012/13 figures. These are a personal tax allowance of £8,105 and 20% tax on income between £8,105 and £42,475.[143] To pay £4,916 in Income Tax, a person needs to earn £32,685: 20% of £32,865 minus the personal tax allowance of £4,916.

---

[141] http://www.hm-treasury.gov.uk/junebudget_diagrams.htm
[142] http://www.ons.gov.uk/ons/taxonomy/index.html?nscl=Population
[143] http://www.hmrc.gov.uk/rates/it.htm

In 2010/11, 25% of people earned £32,910. This means that in 2010/11, 75% of working adults received more from the government than they contributed in tax.

Given that I assumed a 50-yr working life, people who start work later, experience a break in work or retire earlier will need to earn more each year in order to pay off their share of government expenditure.

Appendix 2:
Out-of-date LiMA statements

The following are extracts from two judges' assessments of LiMA and its use by health care professionals in the assessment of Incapacity Benefit claimants. They highlight some of the problems that occur when this system is not set up or used in a manner that will accurately reflect the claimant's health and ability to work.

"The use of this system, in which statements or phrases appear to be capable of being produced mechanically without necessarily representing actual wording chosen and typed in by the examining doctor, obviously carries an increased risk of accidental discrepancies or mistakes remaining undetected in the final product."[144]

"I am afraid I have less of a sense of humour than the tribunal. I do not find it in any way amusing that a formal report of this kind contains the following statements:

- Usually sits to watch TV for 1 hour(s) for about two hours before having to move.
- Usually can do light gardening for 1 minutes.

If that is evidence of anything, it is of Dr A's inattention to what he or she was doing. Nor do I find it amusing that the absurd statement about watching television is repeated word for word in five other places in the report without any of them being corrected. The tribunal was fully justified in rejecting this report as unreliable. Mrs E was fully justified in having no confidence in it.

Having seen a number of these reports, it is clear to me that there is an automated selective carry forward of phrases from Box 7 to the individual boxes for mental health descriptors. For example, the absurd comment about watching television turns up in identical wording in

[144] CIB/551/2005 http://www.osscsc.gov.uk/Aspx/view.aspx?id=1806

boxes 34, 37, 39, 47 and 49 (although I am not sure of its relevance to some of those descriptors). But it does not turn up in boxes 33 or 36 where it might, if properly observed, be relevant."[145]

Many other examples often cited on the internet are taken from the Rights Net Forum, specifically from an archived discussion in June-July 2008.[146] Whilst these examples, with the above judges' comments, highlight the problems that have occurred with LiMA, these come from Incapacity Benefit, not Employment and Support Allowance. The computer programme has been improved since then, on the recommendation of Professor Harrington, and it is to be hoped that such nonsenses are no longer generated. It is therefore not helpful for current disability campaigners to cite examples from the precursor to ESA as reflections on the ESA assessment process.

[145] CIB/664/2005 http://www.osscsc.gov.uk/Aspx/view.aspx?id=1855
[146] http://www.rightsnet.org.uk/forum-archive/index791c-2.html

Printed in the UK by Print On Demand Worldwide, Peterborough.